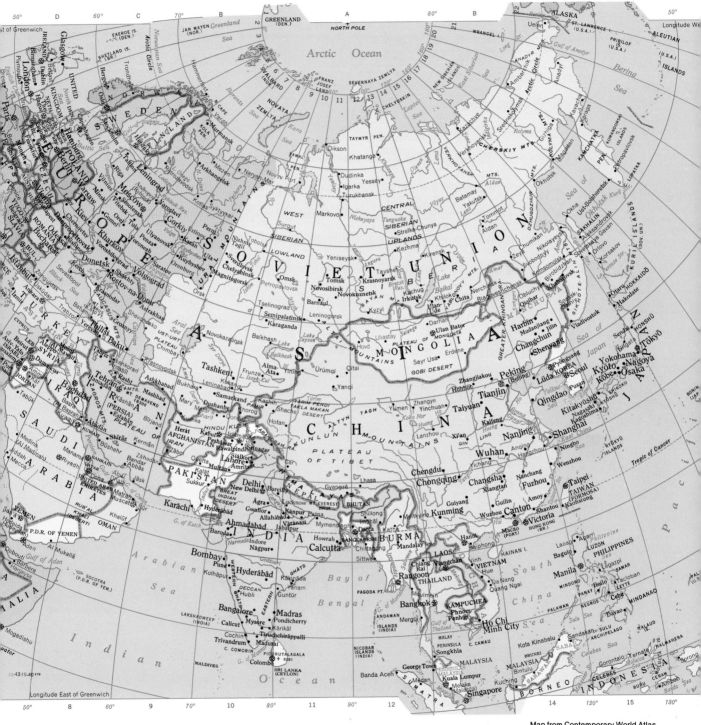

Map from Contemporary World Atlas
© 1992 by Rand McNally, R.L. 92-S-85

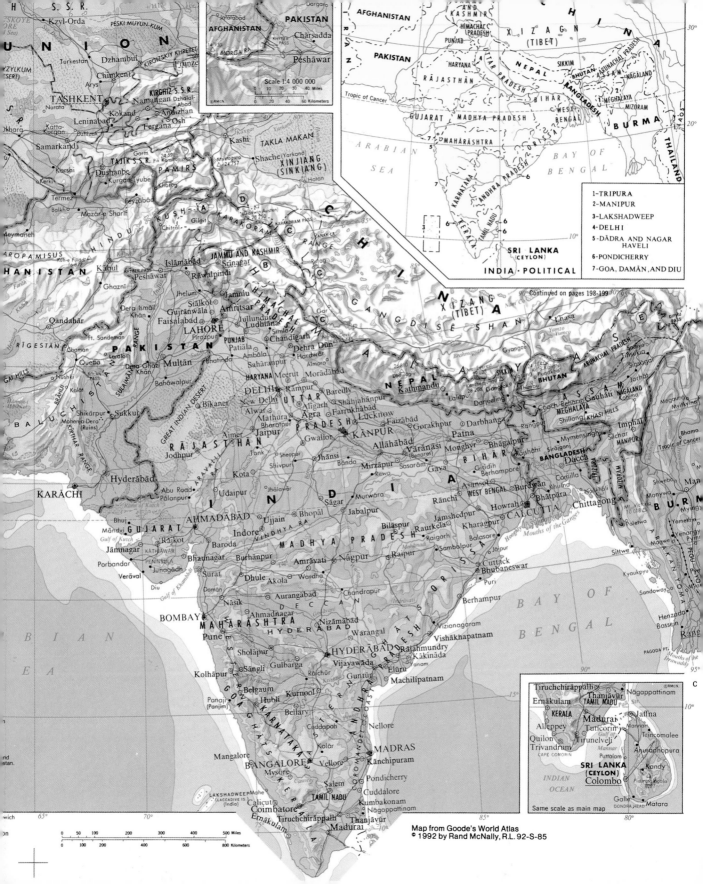

Map from Goode's World Atlas
© 1992 by Rand McNally, R.L. 92-S-85

Enchantment of the World

BANGLADESH

By Jason Lauré

Consultant for Bangladesh: Joan D. Winship, M.A., Augustana College, Department of Political Science, Rock Island, Illinois

Consultant for Reading: Robert L. Hillerich, Ph.D., Visiting Professor, University of South Florida; Consultant, Pinellas County Schools, Florida

CHILDRENS PRESS®
CHICAGO

Bananas are brought to Dhaka in country boats.

Project Editor: Mary Reidy
Design Director: Margrit Fiddle

Library of Congress Cataloging-in-Publication Data

Lauré, Jason.
  Bangladesh / by Jason Lauré.
    p.   cm. — (Enchantment of the world)
  Includes index.
  Summary: An introduction to the geography, history,
economy, culture, and people of Bangladesh, the small,
densely populated neighbor of India.
  ISBN 0-516-02609-7
  1. Bangladesh—Juvenile literature. 2. Bangladesh.
I. Title.
DS393.4.L38 1992   92-8891
954.92—dc20   CIP
                                                   AC

Picture Acknowledgments
AP/Wide World Photos: 14, 15 (inset), 16, 30 (2 photos),
33 (left), 34 (left), 38 (left), 41, 43, 45, 98 (2 photos), 101,
109; **Unicef/Masud Ali,** 13
© **John Elk III:** Cover Inset, 6 (bottom), 78 (right), 90 (top
left & right)
© **Arvind Garg:** 4, 51 (left), 55 (right), 82, 89 (left), 90
(bottom left & right), 91, 92 (2 photos)

© **Virginia R. Grimes:** 65 (bottom left)
Historical Pictures Service/Chicago: 21, 23 (2 photos), 27
Impact Visuals: © **1991 Fuminori Sato,** 15; © **Sean
Sprague,** 55 (left), 66 (2 photos), 80, 94, 111; © **Pam
Hasegawa,** 57 (bottom right), 95, 96 (left); © **Eliason/Link,**
107 (left)
Lauré Communications: © **Jason Lauré,** 6 (top), 8, 33
(right), 34 (right), 37 (right), 38 (right), 39 (2 photos), 48
(top and bottom), 50, 51 (right), 53, 56, 57 (left & top
right), 58 (2 photos), 60 (3 photos), 61 (2 photos), 62 (2
photos), 63, 64 (left), 70 (bottom left & right), 75 (left), 78
(left), 86 (right), 88 (center), 93, 97, 107 (right)
Photri, 9, 84
© **Carl Purcell:** Cover, 70 (top left & right), 73 (left &
center), 75 (right), 84 (inset), 86 (left), 88 (left & right)
Reuters/Bettman: 47
© **Pam Hasegawa,** 5, 10, 70 (center), 73 (top & bottom
right), 77 (2 photos), 79, 89 (right), 96 (right)
Tom Stack & Associates: © **E.P.I. Nancy Adams,** 59 (left);
© **Brian Parker,** 59 (center); © **Gary Milburn,** 64 (right);
© **Mike Severns,** 65 (top left)
UPI/Bettmann: 36 (2 photos), 37 (left), 42, 48 (top), 52
Valan: © **Fred Bavendam,** 59 (right), 65 (bottom right);
© **K. Ghani,** 65 (top right); © **John Cancalosi,** 68 (left);
© **Jean Sloman,** 68 (right); © **Robert C. Simpson,** 69
Len W. Meents: Maps on 10, 21, 91
**Courtesy Flag Research Center, Winchester,
Massachusetts 01890:** Flag on page 6 (inset) and back
cover
Cover: Dhaka
Cover Inset: Dhaka, Burhi Ganga River

Young family members entertain with drums, tambourine, and a table harmonium.

TABLE OF CONTENTS

Above: Most people use bicycle rickshaws to get around in Dhaka.
Below: The countryside near Dhaka

Chapter 1

THE NATURAL
ENVIRONMENT

GEOGRAPHY

Bangladesh, land of the Bengal people, is a small country in
Asia situated in the northeast corner of the Indian subcontinent.
The country measures 55,598 square miles (143,999 square
kilometers) — about the same size as the state of Wisconsin or a
little smaller than the country of Japan. Packed into that space are
118 million people, making Bangladesh the eighth most-populous
country in the world. It also is one of the most densely populated.
More people live on each square mile of land in Bangladesh than
they do almost anywhere else.

Bangladesh faces the Bay of Bengal to the south and is nearly
surrounded on its other three sides by India. A small portion of
the southeastern part of the country is bordered by Burma. The
coastline measures approximately 357 miles (575 kilometers)
along the Bay of Bengal and is very irregular and changeable
according to the season. The country measures 288 miles (463
kilometers) from east to west and 464 miles (747 kilometers) from
north to south.

Much of the land is a flat alluvial plain called the Plain of
Bengal. A small area of the country is hilly. This region, the

The Chittagong Hill Tracts region

Chittagong Hill Tracts, is located in the southeast, bordering
Burma. The highest point there, Mount Keokradong, rises to 4,034
feet (1,230 meters).

RIVERS

Water rules many aspects of life in Bangladesh, which is nestled
within a network of rivers, all flowing southward into the Bay of
Bengal. In the southwestern portion of the land known as the
Sundarbans, water and land are in a constant ebb and flow with
the tides. But elsewhere in Bangladesh, the extreme flatness of the
land and its low position in relation to the sea cause the rivers to
overflow their banks annually.

Although there are an estimated seven hundred rivers, large
and small, flowing through Bangladesh, three river systems
dominate the land. The Ganges enters Bangladesh from the west
and flows southeast. The Jamuna-Brahmaputra flows from the

The Ganges River

north and meets the Ganges not far from the capital city, Dhaka. This combined river continues on its journey under a new name, the Padma. The third river, the Meghna, flows from the northeast border with India until it meets the Padma. Many tiny rivers, called tributaries, spread like fingers all over the southern half of the country. Eventually, all the waters flow into the Bay of Bengal.

The courses of these rivers often shift as they flow because the land is so flat. During the monsoon flood season, rain falls so quickly and with such intensity that the water rushes downstream, leaping out of old river channels. A river may cut itself a new channel and change course. This is one way land is lost in Bangladesh—the river simply takes it over. The old channel is left behind, and anyone who was expecting water from the river's old channel simply can't count on it anymore. Little islands, called *chars*, form, followed almost immediately by the char people. As soon as a char emerges from the water, these people move onto it because land is so scarce and there are so

Aerial view of the river system near Dhaka

many people—although legally they are not allowed to do so. Although it is very dangerous, people will move onto the new land, where the river used to flow. Desperate for land, the char people take a chance. The old riverbed has very fertile soil for farming and the people hope that they and their crops will not be lost during the next monsoon season—that the channel will not be reclaimed by the river. The next monsoon rain often washes away these chars, along with the people living on them.

Because land is so precious and so scarce in Bangladesh, every acre taken out of cultivation is a personal loss for someone who could use it to grow food or jute—a plant whose fibers are made into string or woven into cloth. Since three-quarters of the crops are grown during the monsoon season, the impact of flooding is even more serious.

The rivers divide the land into three areas: Dhaka, Khulna, and Rajshahi. The Chittagong Hill Tracts form a fourth part of the country that connects with the rest of the land only at one narrow point, less than twenty miles (thirty-two kilometers) wide. These natural separations not only divide Bangladesh geographically, they also form the divisions for the administrative sections of the country.

WEATHER

Weather in Bangladesh is often marked by extremes. Rain occurs in the form of monsoons, exceptionally heavy rains that occur on a daily basis during the wet season, usually from late May to the middle of October. During this period, the country receives about 80 percent of the entire year's rainfall. From 55 inches to 235 inches (140 to 597 centimeters) of rain fall over Bangladesh, the most occurring in the northeastern part of the country. Bangladesh has the heaviest rainfall area in the world.

In Bangladesh, as in many tropical countries, seasons are measured as much by rainfall as by temperature. Temperatures are quite mild throughout the year. The summer months of April and May are the hottest, and the monsoon months from June to October are the wettest. The winters are brief, from November to February, with the temperature rarely dropping below 45 degrees Fahrenheit (7.2 degrees Celsius). Humidity is high throughout the year but rises to more than 90 percent in the rainy season; this, combined with temperatures of 100 degrees Fahrenheit (37.7 degrees Celsius), makes the air seem much hotter and makes it difficult to breathe.

Cyclones—storms with high winds and heavy rains, often accompanied by great surges of seawater—cause tremendous damage to the land, the people, and their homes. The center of a cyclone is a spiral of wind that whips around. As it swirls, the spiral of wind builds a mass of air that sucks up water and pushes it ahead like a solid wall. It is this deadly combination of wind and water that causes such devastation in Bangladesh. Occurring on an irregular basis, cyclones form during two periods, from April to May and from September to November.

FLOODS

Flooding is a natural phenomenon that occurs when there is more rainfall than the rivers can carry or the land can absorb. In most parts of the world, flooding is an unusual event because most rivers normally are able to hold the rain that falls and drains into them. In Bangladesh, flooding is *normal*, a yearly event that occurs mainly because of the monsoon rains. Even Dhaka, the capital city, is flooded regularly. After the city's airport was forced to close during the 1988 flood, the government finally took some action and built embankments around it to prevent its closing during future flooding.

In addition to flooding caused by the heavy rainfall, the rivers that flow through Bangladesh are on the last leg of their journey from the nations to the north. They carry the accumulated water from rain that falls in India, Nepal, China, and Bhutan. The water is carried through Bangladesh on the floodplain traversed by the Ganges, the Brahmaputra, and the Meghna, and the numerous tributaries of those rivers. Because most of Bangladesh is flat and because most of it lies barely a few feet above sea level, there is nowhere for the water to go when the monsoons come. Farmers' fields lie underwater when the rivers overflow their banks. With both the normal monsoon rains and the cyclones, floods often occur over a total of six months of the year.

Getting through the streets of Dhaka was difficult after the monsoon rains of August 1988.

During the worst flooding in 1988, considerable areas of Bangladesh were flooded for more than a month. More than 60 percent of the entire country was damaged. Streets and roads disappeared under the water, and whole areas turned into lakes. The water flooded over the fields and destroyed the crops. Nearly 10 percent of the rice crop in Bangladesh was lost that year. Many precious farm animals were drowned, a serious loss for people who count on oxen to plow their fields. The water streamed into

Motorized vehicles were not the preferred means of transportation during the flood.

the houses and stayed there because there was no way for it to drain away.

When the water finally did drain away, there was a great deal of damage to be repaired. Many embankments that were built up along the riverbanks had been washed away and needed to be replaced. Several hundred bridges had been damaged or washed away as torrents of water rushed down the rivers. And more than three million homes were destroyed.

A bridge in Chittagong that was damaged by the cyclone in 1991. Army helicopters brought food into areas destroyed by the cyclone (left).

CYCLONES

Flooding also occurs in Bangladesh as a result of cyclones that form along the coast of the Bay of Bengal.

On November 12, 1970, a cyclone hit Bangladesh (then known as East Pakistan). It was the worst natural disaster in anyone's memory. It was said to be the worst such storm in the area in centuries. So many people were swept away by the violent wind and tide that the exact number will never be known. Most people think at least one-quarter million or possibly one-half million people died that day.

In such a terrible time it is natural for the people to look to their government for assistance; but at this time, the people couldn't count on their government. Yahya Khan, the president of Pakistan (who was responsible for the people in both East Pakistan and

Some of the damage from the 1991 cyclone

West Pakistan), didn't seem to care very much about the situation of the people. In the year to come the people would show their feelings in the voting booths.

The 1970 cyclone stirred up a great deal more than just high wind and rain. It proved to be a pivotal event in the creation of the nation of Bangladesh.

The cyclone of 1991 caused less loss of life, but it came at a time when the country was already suffering from many other problems. Most of these were caused by a lack of money and resources to help the great number of people in need.

On the night of April 29-30, 1991, the cyclone struck the flat coastline of Bangladesh. About 139,000 people died. The loss of property, especially livestock, resulted in the worst long-term damage. In the years between these cyclones, a handful of concrete shelters had been built. While they did help save lives, they had no impact on the loss of homes, livestock, and crops.

Many people never return to their farms after these floods. Sometimes their land just disappears because the courses of the rivers change after such heavy flooding. Once the land is gone, there is no way to bring it back. These farmers become landless, a condition that is a growing problem for Bangladesh, where most of the people still support themselves through agriculture.

CONTROLLING THE ENVIRONMENT

Because all the rivers originate in the north, beyond the borders of Bangladesh, the best way to control the flow would be through a series of storage dams built in other countries. Unfortunately, those other countries have been unwilling to work with Bangladesh to create such a system. So the people must do what they can with the water when it reaches their land. In an *average* year, about one-fifth of the country is flooded.

In recent years, the flow of water rushing down the rivers and over the land has intensified because of the loss of forests to the north. As the forests are cut down, mainly for use as fuel, the water simply floods over the land because there is nothing to slow it down.

A basic way to limit flooding is by building up embankments along the edges of rivers. Such embankments control the amount of water that remains on the land after the heaviest rainfalls by allowing it to drain away safely into the rivers. The water must then be kept somewhere so that it may be used by the farmers for irrigation during the dry season. Without this kind of protection, farmland is either too wet or too dry. For a poor country like Bangladesh, it is difficult to find enough money to spend on these large-scale solutions.

BUILDING A DIKE

A remarkable example of what people can do with their bare hands was demonstrated in a part of Bangladesh where the Feni River flows into the Bay of Bengal. In 1987 hundreds of workers, led by a Dutch engineer, created a dike with sandbags. After filling thousands of sandbags with clay, they waited for the day when the tide was at its absolute lowest. Then, racing against the clock, they piled up the sandbags, layer upon layer, until they had closed the gap across the riverbed. It took 600,000 sandbags to create the embankment. When the tide came back in, the dike held. Once the dike was secure, a reservoir and gates were built to allow water to be released when it was needed in the fields. The farmers also were able to plant a second crop, using the water that was held in reserve.

ANOTHER IRRIGATION PROBLEM

In the southwest portion of the country, the variation in water levels creates a different problem. Because a dam has been built on the Ganges River in India, the amount of water flowing downstream into Bangladesh during the dry season has been severely reduced. This allows water from the Bay of Bengal to move upstream and causes the water in the Ganges to become salty. This water is becoming too salty to use for crop irrigation.

Chapter 2

BENGALI PEOPLE AND LAND

THE FIRST SETTLERS

Bangladesh joined the community of nations as an independent country on December 16, 1971, but the Bengali people and the land on which they live are part of an ancient culture and tradition. The earliest people known to have lived in what is now Bangladesh were the Bang people. They arrived in the area about 1000 B.C., after being driven out of their own homeland to the north.

Several empires were established and spread over the land of India as well as the countries today known as Pakistan and Bangladesh, including the Mauryan Empire (321-185 B.C.), the Gupta Empire (A.D. 320-499), and the Harsha Empire (A.D. 606-647). It was only after the Harsha period that a stable government was established by Gopala, a Buddhist chief. This era was known as the Pala Dynasty (A.D. 750-1150). During most of this period, the rulers practiced the religion of Buddhism. Toward the end of the Pala Dynasty, new leaders who followed the Hindu religion took over.

The population of the land of Bangladesh in those centuries was quite small. Settlement was naturally limited by the violent weather that has always been the dominant fact of life in the area.

TURKISH CONQUEST

Bengal was one of the tribal names first used for the area. Present-day Bangladesh was ruled as a province for several centuries before the Turkish conquest. Eastern Bengal was a political entity as early as A.D. 320 under the *Gupta* (Indian) Empire. When the Buddhist chief Gopala took over as ruler of the Pala Dynasty (A.D. 750-1150), he ruled Bengal as a province or division of his territory. The Pala Dynasty was replaced by *Senas* (Hindus), who ruled until the Turks took over.

Turkish rule was finally established in Bengal in 1202 when the last important Hindu ruler was ousted. The area was basically independent at this point, but maintained its independence in part by paying a tribute (a payment of goods or money for peace or protection) to the Delhi sultan, a Muslim king in India. By about 1350 Bengal became independent from Delhi, and the city of Dhaka was its seat of government. Then, in 1576, Dhaka was conquered by the army of Akbar the Great, the Mughal emperor. Bengal remained under Mughal control for nearly two hundred years, but Dhaka was allowed to function as the provincial (district) capital.

During this period, Bengal enjoyed a kind of independence. Its remote location, far away from Delhi where the government was centered, allowed local officials to run things as they chose. At the same time, Bengal developed its own lively culture and was known for its religious leaders. This uniqueness and strength of

Akbar the Great

character are important reasons why the Bengali people and their nation have been able to survive conditions that would defeat many other people.

When the Turks began their rule, they introduced the people to their religion, Islam. The spread of Islam throughout the area began in the thirteenth century. A whole village would be "converted" to Islam by a Turkish ruler but it took centuries before most of the people living in these villages actually adopted the religion.

The Bengali people lived in the region known as West Bengal (now the state of West Bengal in India) and in East Bengal, which eventually became Bangladesh. This whole region was a rich cultural center that developed quite independently of the rest of the subcontinent though it was all under foreign rule. Turkish rule gave way to the Mughal Empire when Dhaka was conquered in 1576. The Bengal region remained part of the Mughal Empire until the eighteenth century.

While under the control of the Mughals, Bengal developed two fundamental factors of its economy. Its agriculture, based on fertile land and an abundance of rainfall, enabled it to feed much of India. At the same time, the agricultural industry grew into a thriving and prosperous occupation for many people.

The vast distance between Delhi and Dhaka (about 1,000 miles; 1,609 kilometers) convinced the governors to move the provincial capital of Bengal to Murshidabad in India in 1704. This had the effect of making Bengal more independent because it now had even less contact with the Mughal government.

ARRIVAL OF THE EUROPEANS

The isolation of Bengal and the difficulty of land travel made it inevitable that when European traders arrived in the seventeenth century, they would do so by sea. Although Europeans had been trading with the Indian subcontinent (present-day India, Pakistan, and Bangladesh), they had to rely on Arab merchants who were able to travel overland. In time, the Europeans grew suspicious of these traders, believing that they were charging too much for their services; they decided to look for their own trade routes to India. The Portuguese began sailing to Bengal in the sixteenth century, settling near the port of Chittagong; by the seventeenth century, some had moved to Dhaka.

It was the British East India Company, formed in 1600, that established the first important trade with Bengal. The company arrived just about the time the Mughals were losing power and so, instead of just being involved in the business aspects of Bengal,

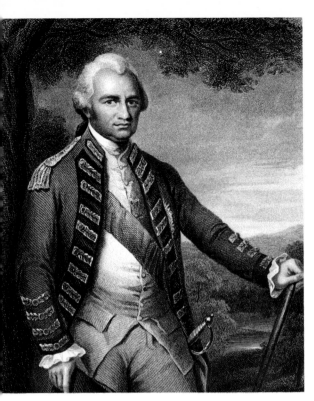

Robert Clive, an official of the British East India Company (left), and native officers and soldiers employed by the company (above)

the company became directly involved in its politics and military matters. The British East India Company founded the city of Calcutta in Bengal in 1690. Calcutta became one of the most important cities for the British during their reign in India and it later served as their capital.

When the governor of Bengal, Siraj ud Daulah, attacked the British in 1757, he was defeated by Robert Clive, an official of the British East India Company. The company became the tax collector in Bengal, as well as in the neighboring territories of Bihar and Orissa, because all of this region was part of India. This was the beginning of British control over all of India (including the areas that came to be Pakistan and Bangladesh). The British East India Company often became the ruling force in a foreign country, acting on its own behalf, rather than that of the British government. But it paved the way for the British government to take over such areas, and so it was in Bengal. By 1784 the company was acting directly on behalf of the British government and reporting to Parliament. Many of the problems that exist in Bangladesh today can be traced directly back to the changes made by the British East India Company.

THE BRITISH RAJ

The British rule over the Indian subcontinent is known as the *Raj*. India, which included Pakistan and Bangladesh, was called "the jewel in the crown." It was seen as the most precious of the nations that formed the Commonwealth, the group of nations ruled by Great Britain. But that rule was often inappropriate, and sometimes totally thoughtless—as in the change the British introduced in the system of tax collection.

Before the British came, the tax collectors, called *zamindars*, acted as local magistrates. But under the new system, the right to collect taxes was sold to the man with the most money. Because the land that was taxed was used for farming, it was important for the tax collector to be familiar with agriculture. As the land was sold to people who didn't need it for farming, more and more families found themselves unable to afford to have their own land to farm. The people who owned more land than they needed were able to live well. They sold the extra food they produced to those who could afford to buy it. However, they did not grow enough food to make up for all the people who were forced off their land.

Often, the new landowners lived far away. They hired peasant farmers to work the land for them, but these farmers had no interest in getting the most out of the land. They never benefited from the profits that went to the absentee landlords. Not surprisingly, the nation's ability to produce food suffered. The British didn't have bad intentions when they introduced the system; it was the same system that was used at home. But everything in India was different: the land, the people, the crops. The British were so sure their system was right, they overlooked all these differences. The problem of the absentee landlord still stands in the way of efficient food production in Bangladesh.

CHANGING A CULTURE

The British, however, did not always simply *overlook* cultural differences. Sometimes, they decided to change the values that the people treasured, to make them more like the English. To do this they began to change the school curriculum. Relatively few children went to school. As students proceeded into the higher grades, they were taught in English, rather than in their own language. By turning the more-educated people into English speakers, the British were more easily able to impose their own cultural beliefs on the people they ruled. They also changed the language of government from Persian, which the Mughals used, to English. They created a sense that being "British" or like the British had a higher moral value than being "Indian." At the same time, the British viewed their colonies as suppliers of raw materials, not as producers of finished products.

Although Bengal had a thriving textile industry of its own, and was exporting both muslin and fine silk to Europe by the eighteenth century, Great Britain saw more value in the Bengalis as consumers of fabrics produced in England. To force the people to buy British cloth, they "dumped" it onto the local markets at prices that were lower than that of locally made cloth. In a short time, the homespun cloth of Dhaka became unsalable and the textile industry was destroyed.

THE FIRST UPRISING

The unhappiness of the people due to the many changes made by the British finally erupted in conflict. On May 10, 1857, soldiers mutinied near Delhi in India. The revolt is known by several names: the Sepoy Rebellion, the Great Mutiny, and the Revolt of 1857. These troops, mostly Muslim, were surrounded on June 20, 1858. The British government saw that it was time to end the role played by the British East India Company. Great Britain now assumed direct rule, beginning the era called the British Raj. The colony was known as British India and was ruled by a governor-general.

THE RISE OF NATIONALISM

At the time of the revolt, India was also home to many little states, called princely states. These princely states remained independent of the British Raj while others began to work more closely with the British. There was no feeling of being one nation or one country. To the Muslims of Bengal, however, it was clear that they never did as well as the Hindus, the other religion of the region. Most positions of power were held by Hindus, and the money that was earned was spent by Hindus. It seemed to the Muslims that the more they worked, the richer the Hindus became. At the same time, the education the Muslims received kept them apart from the Hindus. Even when the British imposed their system of education, the number of children who attended school was quite low; there weren't enough teachers even for those who wanted to go to school. The Muslims preferred to teach their own values to their children in religious schools, and this widened the gap between them and the Hindus, who quickly adapted to the British system.

George Curzon

Chapter 3

PARTITION

BENGAL IS DIVIDED

In 1905 the land of Bengal was divided into two sections, the east and the west, by the British governor-general, Lord George Curzon. He decided that a new province, East Bengal, should be established with the ancient city of Dhaka as its capital. Then he created the new province of West Bengal whose capital was Calcutta, the city established in 1690 by the British East India Company. While this pleased the Bengali Muslims, it displeased the Hindus of Calcutta. They argued against the division so effectively that by 1912 the British gave in and the two parts of Bengal were reunited.

In 1885 the Indian National Congress was organized as an all-Indian political organization. Although there were Muslim members, it was dominated by Hindus. The Muslims, however, wanted to find a way to protect their own interests. The All-India Muslim League, formed in 1906, continued to press for the rights of its people throughout India. Bitter feelings between the two groups continued through the decades that followed.

Throughout recent history, various rulers have tried to solve the problems of the region by dividing the land in different ways. They drew lines on maps and declared that one area would belong to one group of people and another area would belong to a different group of people. People, of course, are rarely divided up so neatly, and inevitably, many people wound up moving or being moved from one area to another to make these divisions more nearly true. The idea of a separate state for Muslims surfaced in 1930 in a speech given by Sir Muhammad Iqbal. He believed that the Muslims had a legitimate claim to be a nation.

TWO NATIONS

During the 1930s, the leader of the Muslim League, Mohammad Ali Jinnah, continued to press for a Muslim state, to be called *Pakistan*. The name had been created by a group of students by combining the first letters of the names of various sections of the northwest portion of India. The country, Pakistan, was meant to include the Muslims of northwest India, but not the people of Bengal, so many miles away. In 1940, the Muslim League proposed that the state include the areas where Muslims were in the majority, which included both the northwest and the northeast portion of India. The northeast was Bengal. The split between the Muslims and Hindus grew wider.

Throughout this period, the British ruled almost all of India, which was still considered a colony. The British opposed independence for India entirely because more of the independence leaders were Hindu and the British wanted to keep India together. The Muslims maintained better relations with the British than did the Hindus. For more than twenty years, Mohandas K. Gandhi, a

Hindu and the leading figure in the Indian National Congress, fought against British rule over India. The Muslim leader Ali Jinnah opposed Gandhi, and the two sides continued to feud.

When Britain decided to give India its independence, it was largely because Britain's ability to govern there had declined so sharply. The British would have been forced to maintain control by using their armed forces and, with India's huge population, this was not a practical solution.

Various ideas were considered regarding the form of India's independence, and in 1946, elections were held that were to lead to self-government. Although the Muslim League won 90 percent of the seats in Muslim areas, the Muslims still were not given adequate representation. At first Jinnah called for demonstrations against the interim government, but the rioting that followed forced him to change his plan and he brought the Muslim League into the interim government. Ultimately the interim government was not an effective force. The Muslims demanded a role in the government that was equal to that of the Indian National Congress. This demand was unrealistic because the Muslims were a minority in the country.

INDIA INDEPENDENCE ACT

In 1947 the viceroy of India was Lord Louis Mountbatten. He quickly moved to create a plan for almost immediate independence for all of India. The British House of Commons fulfilled this plan by passing the India Independence Act on July 14, 1947. It became known as the Partition because it divided the land of India into two countries. Most of the land was apportioned to India. To the east and the west of India, two wings

Above: Mohandas K. Gandhi, a Hindu, opposed partition of India. Left: Mohammad Ali Jinnah, in white (talking with Louis Mountbatten, Viceroy of India), thought the Indian Muslims should separate from the rest of India.

of land were sectioned off to create the east and west parts of Pakistan. There was very little thought given to the way the country would succeed with its two halves separated by 1,000 miles (1,609 kilometers). Trying to separate the people of India who followed the Hindu religion from those who were Muslims, officials simply drew lines around the areas where the largest concentrations of Muslims lived. The areas that resulted were East Pakistan and West Pakistan.

The idea to divide the country actually came from the leader of the Muslim League, Mohammad Ali Jinnah. He believed that the Muslims in India would be able to resolve differences among themselves if they were joined together and separated from the rest of India. Jinnah became the governor-general of the new Dominion of Pakistan in August 1947.

PARTITION

Partition proved to be an apt description of the new nation of Pakistan. Everything about it was in parts, each separated from the other and operating against the best interests of its people. The abrupt shift from British control to independence left Pakistan with many shortages, among them people who had experience in running a government. Most of the Muslim businesspeople were centered in West Pakistan.

THE TWO PAKISTANS

Combining two areas as far apart physically, culturally, and temperamentally as East Pakistan and West Pakistan brought with it a built-in tension. The people spoke different languages, had different beliefs and traditions, and came from different ethnic backgrounds. The only common element was their religion: Islam. The business centers, the government, and the armed forces were all established in West Pakistan, although the majority of the population was located in East Pakistan. Despite the greater population, East Pakistan was left out of political decisions and given very little in the way of monetary assistance. East Pakistan was also the crop-producing area where jute, the nation's principal crop, was grown. However, West Pakistan controlled most of the earnings and invested the income in its part of the country at the expense of East Pakistan, which became poorer and poorer. The West Pakistanis developed a vast civil service system that employed many people and enabled them to rule over the Bengalis in East Pakistan. Much of the money earned by the Bengalis went to build up the Pakistan military based in the west. Pakistan waged war against India twice before using the military against its own eastern wing, which ultimately became Bangladesh.

LANGUAGE RIOTS

But aside from the questions of economic inequality, the issue particularly angering the Bengalis concerned language. The people in West Pakistan spoke Urdu, whereas those in East Pakistan spoke Bengali. Since the government was based in West Pakistan, the Bengali-speaking people were at an economic and political disadvantage. When the West Pakistanis declared that Urdu would be the official and only language of the two Pakistans, riots broke out over the language issue and gave the dissatisfaction a clear focus. The fact that the majority of people in the two Pakistans were Bengali speaking was overlooked by the West Pakistanis. They also ignored the people in West Pakistan who spoke other languages: Punjabi, Sindhi, Pushtu, and Baluchi.

The language riots began on February 22, 1952, when students demonstrated against the imposition of Urdu. Two years later, the National Assembly finally declared that Bengali along with Urdu and whatever other languages were needed would be the official languages of Pakistan. Tensions remained high in Pakistan for years, even after the language issue was resolved. Politicians from the two Pakistans fought one another for control of the nation. Through the years, the West Pakistanis maintained effective financial control and continued to use the resources of East Pakistan for their own people's benefit.

SHEIKH MUJIB

When Ayub Khan became president in 1958, the gap between East and West Pakistan grew even wider. But East Pakistan now had its own political leader, Sheikh Mujibur Rahman. Mujib, as

Ayub Khan (left) and Mujibur Rahman (right)

he was known, strongly believed that East Pakistan had to be freed from the domination of Ayub Khan and West Pakistan. Although he was put in jail for his views, Mujib was a fiery person who inspired his people.

Sheikh Mujibur Rahman knew that the Bengali people would always be second-class citizens as long as they were part of Pakistan. By 1966 he had drawn up a program to give the people of East Pakistan control over their political lives. This program was called the Six Points and was outlined in a pamphlet called "Our Right to Live," published by the Awami League, Mujib's political party.

One of the chief grievances was the misuse of money earned in East Pakistan. To address this complaint, one of Mujib's six points stated there should be separate currencies for each of the two

Yahya Khan (left) and Mujib (right) with his advisors

Pakistans and that separate bank accounts should be maintained
as well. Shortly after this program was announced, the
government of Ayub Khan arrested Mujib, along with the other
leaders of the Awami League.

During the nine months he was kept in prison, Mujib's
influence grew; he became a symbol of all the wrongs that West
Pakistan enacted against its east wing. It was clear to the Bengalis
that they would never be truly free until they had their own
country. Mujib was the leader who gave them the hope that this
dream would come true and his actions earned him the name
Bangabandhu—"friend of Bangladesh."

By 1969 Ayub Khan was too ill to continue in office and he
turned the government over to a general, Yahya Khan, who
placed the country under martial law. Elections were scheduled to
be held in December 1970.

Chapter 4

THE BIRTH OF

BANGLADESH

THE CYCLONE

Before the elections were held, a natural disaster occurred, one of such enormous proportions that it actually changed the destiny of the nation and led to the independence of East Pakistan. The event was a cyclone.

On November 12, 1970, with little warning, a cyclone swept in off the Bay of Bengal and hit a huge area of coastal East Pakistan. Reports of the number of lives lost are, perhaps, only guesses, but it is believed that 250,000 people died. Countless others were left homeless. President Yahya Khan stopped briefly in Dhaka on his way home from a trip abroad but showed little interest in helping the people of East Pakistan with food, clothing, or shelter.

Elections were held on December 7, 1970, and the results proved decisively that the majority of the people wanted a change of government. Sheik Mujib's Awami League swept the elections, winning nearly all of the seats allotted to East Pakistan in the National Assembly. If the laws of the nation had been followed, Mujib would have become prime minister of all of Pakistan, because a majority of the population lived in the east. Instead,

Above: Mujib supporters demonstrated at the Pakistan Embassy in Washington, D.C.
Left: Mutilated bodies of intellectuals killed by the army in 1971

Yahya delayed the opening of the National Assembly and ordered masses of troops from West Pakistan to enter East Pakistan. He had decided to use military force to accomplish what the elections had not—the surrender of the people of East Pakistan to the rule of Yahya and his political faction.

MASSACRE

The military's attack began on March 25, 1971, when the Pakistan army began slaughtering people in Dhaka. The primary targets were people at the university, people who represented the intellectual life of East Pakistan as well as the Hindu parts of the city. The army had lists of names and proceeded to kill hundreds of Bengalis. They also arrested Sheikh Mujibur Rahman and flew him to West Pakistan to prison. To be sure news of the massacre did not reach the attention of the world, the army gathered up the

In December 1971 India's Prime Minister Indira Ghandi (right) sent in troops. East Indian freedom fighters sit on an Indian tank (left).

foreign journalists in Dhaka and expelled them from the country. It is thought that more than one million Bengalis were killed during the nine-month war that followed.

It is not really accurate to call most of the action during this period a war because the fighting was done by the army on behalf of West Pakistan and most of the dying was done by the people of East Pakistan. India, caught in the middle, became the temporary home to about ten million refugees who fled across the border from East Pakistan.

It was clear to India's Prime Minister Indira Gandhi that India would have to step in militarily to put an end to the fighting. On December 4, 1971, the Indian army attacked the West Pakistan forces and in just twelve days succeeded in defeating them. They received important help from the freedom fighters of East Pakistan known as the Mukti Bahini. The Mukti Bahini symbolized the fighting spirit of the East Bengali people. Their

Above: Mukti Bahini used weapons made in Czechoslovakia and Bulgaria. Left: People cheer as the flag of independent Bangladesh is raised.

biggest advantage was the support they received from the people, who gave them whatever food and shelter they could. The Mukti Bahini operated with very little in the way of war materials until they were joined by Bengali defectors from the West Pakistan army. India allowed the Mukti Bahini to take sanctuary on its territory and also provided substantial amounts of equipment.

THE BIRTH OF BANGLADESH

The nation of Bangladesh celebrates two birth dates: the first is March 26, 1971, when the nation declared itself to be independent. That was the day after the war against West Pakistan began. However, it was December before any government recognized the new nation that called itself Bangladesh. On December 16, West Pakistan forces surrendered, and that became the second independence day of Bangladesh. The final step in the Partition of India had taken place. Bangladesh—the Bengal nation—was born.

Mujib and members of his government return in triumph (left);
refugees (right) were finally able to return to their country.

Nearly a month later, Sheikh Mujibur Rahman was released
from jail in West Pakistan. He triumphantly returned to Dhaka on
January 10, 1972, to lead a nation that was devastated by the
cyclone and the war, overpopulated, and underfed. But he
returned joyously to the free nation of Bangladesh.

IRON HAND

It is often said that the people who lead a nation to victory are
not the ones who should run the country. In Mujib's case, this
quickly proved to be true. He had been in and out of prison for
twenty years; he had little grasp of the skills needed to lead people
in the day-to-day details of nation building. He had been most
powerful when he was in prison, in isolation. His isolation was so
complete that he did not know his people had elected him
president of Bangladesh, ready for the time when that nation
would, in fact, exist.

Not surprisingly, Mujib trusted those who had supported him and his cause during the war for independence. Appointments to civil service positions—the jobs that run governments on a day-to-day basis—were given to people according to their politics, rather than their skills.

Mujib moved to take control of most of the manufacturing and trading businesses by making them part of the government's operations. This took away people's incentive to set up or maintain the many small companies that make it possible for a country to function. Unfortunately, the government did not have the expertise to manage or operate all these different manufacturing and agricultural companies. And, in a turnabout-is-fair-play notion, he replaced English with Bengali throughout the government and in the schools. This made it virtually impossible for the outside world to deal with Bangladesh on any level. The economic consequences were obvious: the shaky new country began going downhill quickly. Bangladesh's usual struggles with flooding and a shortage of food were intensified by these policies.

Three years after Mujib's release from prison and his hero's welcome, he expanded his powers as president and proclaimed Bangladesh a one-party state. Many basic rights that were written into the constitution no longer applied. On August 15, 1975, Mujib was assassinated by a group of army officers. His popularity had reached such a low point that this former savior of the people was scarcely mourned.

MILITARY RULE

In the tumultuous two years that followed, the country was ruled by the military that had been responsible for Mujib's death.

*President
Zia-ur Rahman
at his first
news conference*

The government was unstable, changing frequently. At the end of
1976, General Zia-ur Rahman, known as Zia, declared himself to
be in charge. He took the position of president a few months later.
Although he took power in an undemocratic change of
government, Zia proved to be a popular leader. He felt so secure
in his genuine popularity that he held a referendum in 1977 so
that the people could declare whether they wanted him to
continue as president. Even though the results of the election were
considered somewhat inflated, it was clear that Zia did have
popular support.

Zia moved to bring Bangladesh back into contact with other
nations, especially those in the Islamic world. Although Zia died
in 1981, his efforts eventually resulted in the formation of the
seven-nation South Asian Association for Regional Cooperation
(SAARC), which was established in 1983. It held its first summit
conference in December 1986, in Bangladesh. It was a mark of
how far the former enemies had come: included in the seven were
Pakistan and India.

President Hussain Muhammad Ershad in 1990, shortly before he was arrested and charged with corruption and illegal possession of firearms

Zia's popularity continued through the next election period, when his party won two-thirds of the seats in Parliament. A little more than two years later, on May 30, 1981, Zia was assassinated by a member of the army. The man thought to be the leader of the plot was also killed.

ERSHAD EMERGES

The new head of government was Zia's vice-president, Abdus Sattar, but he was soon pushed into the background by the head of the army, Major General Hussain Muhammad Ershad. On March 24, 1982, Ershad removed Sattar from power and appointed himself the leader of the country. Once again, the democratic process of the country was pushed aside.

There were many different groups opposed to Ershad, but they were unable to unite in their opposition and he remained in power. Ershad took apart the democratic framework of the nation, suspended the country's constitution, and disbanded Parliament,

An election poster shows Sheikh Hasina Wajed and her father Mujibur Rahman, who was assassinated in 1975.

the governmental body that makes the laws of the country. By the end of 1983, Ershad had *officially* become president; he ruled the country under martial law until the end of 1986.

Growing opposition encouraged the rise of other political leaders, notably Sheikh Hasina Wajed, a daughter of Mujib, and Begum Khaleda Zia, the widow of President Zia. (*Begum* indicates that she is married.) Their parties, as well as many other groups, pushed for an end to martial law and a restoration of the basic rights of citizens. Ershad responded by continuing his strong grip on the country but also by moving the government toward civilian rule, according to his own schedule.

MILITARY RULE EASES

Although still in control, Ershad eased some aspects of martial law and allowed elections in 1986. The voting was believed to be unfair and was marked by fraud and violence, but the results gave Ershad a majority of the seats in Parliament. He then joined the leading party and became its candidate for president. In this way, he maintained control of the country through the military, while giving the appearance of offering democratic, civilian rule. Although the presidential election was widely boycotted, and the results were again believed to be fraudulent, Ershad claimed he was the clear winner with 84 percent of the votes.

Protest against Ershad's rule and his methods continued through the end of the 1980s, including general strikes that disrupted daily life and left some of the strikers dead. By the beginning of 1990, people opposing Ershad's Jatiya party publicly were quite literally taking their lives in their own hands. Rather than simply boycotting the elections as they had in the past, voters belonging to opposition parties began making their anger known. It was clear that Ershad would never win a fair election. As protests grew, increasing numbers of people were killed and wounded during demonstrations. In response to the unrest, Ershad declared a state of emergency.

ERSHAD RESIGNS

By the beginning of December 1990, Ershad's rule had come to an end. Although he had set himself the task of ridding the country of corruption, it was the charge of personal corruption that finally took him from power. He was accused, along with

Ershad was escorted by police guard during his trial.

several aides, of receiving more than $8 million as a result of the government's agreement to purchase planes from British Aerospace. He also was charged with illegal arms possession.

For a brief period Ershad attempted to hold onto his power until the next elections; instead, he was forced to resign on December 6, 1990. He went into hiding in an effort to avoid being arrested but was found and jailed on December 20. From his jail cell he successfully fought to remain on the ballot for parliamentary elections. During the period between his resignation and the elections for a new president, a caretaker government under the country's Chief Justice of the Supreme Court took over.

ELECTIONS 1991

The elections of February 27, 1991, marked a unique moment in the brief history of Bangladesh: they were the first peaceful, democratic elections the people had ever known. Observers applauded the people for holding free and fair elections, an event that they hoped would lead to a new democratic government for the Bengali people. Two major candidates running for leader of Bangladesh were both closely associated with important figures from Bangladesh's past. Begum Khaleda Zia is the widow of former President Zia-ur Rahman, who was assassinated in 1981. Opposing her was Sheikh Hasina Wajed, the daughter of Bangladesh's first president, Sheikh Mujibur Rahman, who was likewise killed while in office. Neither woman was a political figure on her own, but both sparked considerable sympathy from the people because of the way in which the two men were killed. This willingness to elect people to office because of their ties with a former leader is a familiar occurrence in Asia and in Latin America. People often vote out of loyalty for the former leader; in this case, they had a choice between two former leaders.

In the 1991 elections, the widow, Begum Khaleda Zia, had the most votes. Although she did not win a clear majority, she had far more votes than her closest competitor, Sheikh Hasina Wajed. There are 300 seats in the country's Parliament and her party won 140 of those seats. (Thirty seats are reserved for women who are appointed by the ruling party.) A month after the election, a party of strict Muslims, the Jamaat-E-Islami gave their support to the Bangladesh Nationalist party. With their 18 seats, and working under the parliamentary system, Begum Khaleda now had enough seats to become head of government and she was sworn in as prime minister on March 20. (In Bangladesh, because so many people have the same surnames, they are often referred to by their given names.)

Begum Khaleda Zia taking the oath of office

The people had chosen a woman who represented the popular
leadership of her late husband to lead them; her opponent
represented the man who is still considered the father of the
nation, but whose leadership was a grave dissappointment. The
elections were the first in the history of Bangladesh in which a
woman was chosen head of government. They also were the first
in which the voting was seen as free, fair, and unmarked by
violence. Perhaps this could be seen as the rebirth of Bangladesh.

Left: Rabindranath Tagore,
the best-known Indian Bengali
poet, received the Nobel Prize
for Literature in 1913.
Below and above: The language of
Bangladesh, which is derived
from Sanskrit, is written in
a flowing, graceful script.

Chapter 5
CULTURE AND PEOPLE

LANGUAGE AND LITERATURE

Culture is the reason for the existence of Bangladesh. It was the source of its hostile relationship with West Pakistan when the two areas were linked politically as one country. The cultural identity of the Bengalis, their fierce pride in their own language and history, set them apart in many ways from the people of West Pakistan.

It is not surprising that one of the chief monuments in Dhaka is dedicated to those who died in the language riots in 1952. The Bangla, or Bengali, language is the first indication of the individuality of the culture. It is derived from Sanskrit, an ancient language, and is written in a flowing, graceful script. The Bengali people have a special relationship with their own language, and though few are literate, they have a great love of oral traditional literature and poetry. The Bauls of Bengal, religious singers, travel throughout the country singing Bengali ballads.

The strength of the Bengali culture is shared by all Bengali people, whether they are from the state of Bengal in India or the nation of Bangladesh. Indeed, the best-known Bengali writer is Rabindranath Tagore, who was born in Calcutta, in India. He won

The Bangladesh Children's Cultural Troupe

the Nobel Prize for literature in 1913. Tagore's poetry describes all
of Bengal. He often wrote about the beautiful Bengali countryside,
particularly the Ganges River. Tagore is still read and admired as
if he were a contemporary figure, and his song, "Our Golden
Bengal," became Bangladesh's national anthem. Another writer,
Kazi Nazrul Islam, is known as the voice of Bengali nationalism.
The birthdays of Tagore and Nazrul are marked as important and
joyous holidays. Bengali playwrights also have made major world
contributions.

MUSIC AND DANCE

The Bangladesh Children's Cultural Troupe, *Kochi Konther Asar
Bangladesh,* is a group of children who bring the song and dance of
their native land to people around the world. They were part of
the international celebration, the World Summit for Children,
held at the United Nations in September 1990. The children

Left: Advertisements for movies are colorful promotions.
Right: Sarita Choudhury, a Bangladeshi actress, starred with
Denzel Washington in the film Mississippi Masala.

present folk dances as well as modern dances, many of them set to words and music by Tagore and Nazrul. The songs tell of everyday events in Bangladesh and well-known events in the country's history.

FILMS

A lively filmmaking industry in Bangladesh makes films considered suitable for the local market. Most educated Bangladeshis have videotape players, and they choose from the vast assortment of movies made in Western countries.

A Bangladeshi actress, Sarita Choudhury, was chosen to star in a film based on the story of an Indian family living in Uganda, in Africa. They, and 200,000 other Indians, were thrown out of Uganda by the dictator Idi Amin. Many wound up in Mississippi, and their story is told in a film called *Mississippi Masala*. *Masala* is a spicy Bangladesh (Indian) stew. The film was first shown at the Venice Film Festival in Italy, where it was enthusiastically received. It opened in the United States in February 1992.

George Harrison and Eric Clapton gave a concert in 1971 to aid the people of Bangladesh.

CONCERT FOR BANGLADESH

On August 1, 1971, a remarkable live concert was held at Madison Square Garden in New York City to aid the people of Bangladesh. George Harrison of the popular Beatles led the all-star program of musicians, who created an album that stayed on the best-seller charts for forty-one weeks. That concert marked the first time that many people heard about Bangladesh. Through the years, the concert, the album, and a movie made of the concert have earned more than $13 million for Bangladesh.

In 1991, in honor of the twentieth anniversary of the concert and of the birth of Bangladesh, Capitol Records reissued *The Concert for Bangla Desh* album (as it was then spelled), this time in compact disc form. As with the first album, the profits will go to help the children of Bangladesh; the United Nations International Children's Emergency Fund (UNICEF) oversees the distribution.

Playing soccer

SPORTS

The most important spectator sport for the people of Bangladesh is soccer (called "football"), and the highlight of the year is the international championship playoffs—the World Cup matches. People watch the World Cup events on television at home or on communal sets that are placed in village squares. The people cheer for their favorite teams and snap up the official guides published in both English and Bengali. During the 1990 World Cup events, Bangladesh Television broadcast thirty matches live.

On a more active level, Bengalis participate in cricket, a game that came to the country during the British colonial era. A team from Bangladesh competes against teams from other Asian countries: India, Pakistan, Sri Lanka, Malaysia, and Singapore.

MARRIAGE

In Bangladesh, marriages are almost always arranged by the parents, but unlike the custom in some other Muslim countries, the young people can say no to the intended marriage partner. When that happens, the parents then arrange another match. Young people who have a chance to complete their education marry quite late, by Bengali standards—rarely before they are twenty-five years old. There is no pressure to marry young; it is beneficial to put off marriage as long as possible because of the country's enormous population.

TELEVISION

Television programming in Bangladesh is a combination of traditional Bengali culture and popular western shows, particularly American programs. A week's programming recently offered such familiar shows as "Wonderful World of Disney," the "Bill Cosby Show," and "Miami Vice," along with a daily reading from the Koran, the holy book of Islam; "Songs of Tagore," Bengal's best-known poet; news in English; and programs in the Bengali language. During one week in June 1990, the feature every day was a live broadcast of international teams competing in World Cup soccer.

THE RELIGION OF ISLAM

Bangladesh is officially known as a Muslim nation and was declared so by former President Ershad. About 80 to 85 percent of the people are Muslims. Although some Islamic nations are very

Above: The Sitara (star) Mosque in Dhaka
Left: A boy studying the Koran

strict in their practices, the people of Bangladesh—although devout—do not impose their religious views on others, and religious rituals are much more relaxed. Women, for example, do not have to cover their faces in public or wrap themselves up in garments to conceal their bodies, as is the practice in some Arabic-Islamic countries. Bangladeshis have adapted the Islamic religion to their own culture, especially in the rural areas.

Muslims are required to pray five times a day, kneeling on the ground, then bending down until their heads touch the earth. They face Mecca, the holiest city of Islam, while they are praying. Men often are seen gathered in huge groups, row after row on the ground, bowing down in unison. Women usually pray at home; when they do attend prayer services, they are separated from the men in the mosques, the Muslim places of worship.

During Eid al Fitr *it is a tradition to give money to beggars.*

RAMADAN

The holiest time of the Islamic year is the observance of Ramadan, a period during which everyone who is physically able does not eat or drink during the entire day, every day, for a month. Each night, as soon as the sun sets, people rush home for the meal that breaks the fast. Because the Muslim calendar follows the phases of the moon, rather than the sun, the period of Ramadan falls at different seasons in different years.

At the end of the month of fasting, everyone waits eagerly for the sight of the new moon, the indication that Ramadan is over. This is celebrated with the feast of *Eid al Fitr.*

OTHER RELIGIONS

The Bangladeshis are quite tolerant of other religions. The proportion of Hindus in Bangladesh has changed dramatically

*In Bangladesh different religions are tolerated. Buddhists (left),
Hindus (top right), and Christians (right) can practice openly.*

over the years, as Hindus moved out and then back into
Bangladesh. Today, Hindus make up about 15 percent of the
population; like the Muslims in Bangladesh, Hindus observe
rituals that are unique to them. One of the principal differences
between Hindus and Muslims is that each Hindu is considered a
member of a particular caste, a social class into which he or she is
born. This automatically makes some Hindus superior to others.
Muslims, however, believe that every person is equal.

The people of the Chittagong Hill Tracts, who are culturally
quite different from the Bengalis, follow the Buddhist religion.
Fewer than a million people throughout Bangladesh are
Christians.

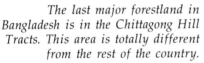
The last major forestland in Bangladesh is in the Chittagong Hill Tracts. This area is totally different from the rest of the country.

THE CHITTAGONG HILL TRACTS

The southeastern region of Bangladesh, known as the Chittagong Hill Tracts, is completely different from the rest of the country in every way imaginable. It is only because of a land surveyor's pen that this region was incorporated into Bangladesh. Geographically and tribally, it belongs to Burma to the east. The land is mountainous, not flat. The Chittagong Hill Tracts is the site of the last major forestland in Bangladesh. The forest survives because of the relatively small number of people who live on the land. Though the people use bamboo plants for building homes and for fuel, the plants are not used up faster than they can be replenished. Teak is an important product of these forests.

The few elephants that still remain in Bangladesh are found here, often employed in moving timber. These are the Asian

The Asian elephant (far left), the rare and endangered clouded leopard (left), and the python (above) are found in the Chittagong Hill Tracts.

elephants, which are different from the African elephants. The Asian elephant is smaller and has much smaller ears. Its nature is different too, making it possible to tame and train these elephants for labor.

Some wildcats are said to inhabit these hills as well, including the very rare and endangered clouded leopard. Pythons inhabit the land near the riverbanks.

TRIBAL ANCESTRY

The tribal people of the Chittagong Hill Tracts are not of Bengali ancestry and do not speak the Bengali language. They number fewer than one million, represent at least a dozen different tribes, and speak as many languages. The major tribal peoples are the Chakma, the Tippera, the Marma, and the Mru.

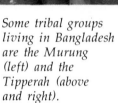

Some tribal groups living in Bangladesh are the Murung (left) and the Tipperah (above and right).

The people's faces reveal their ancestry at once: these are the faces of Burma and Mongolia, with their wide features and light-brown skin. Each tribe wears distinctive clothing, often of fabric handwoven by the people, and the women wear necklaces that drape around their necks like bibs. The pottery and fabrics they make are among the most popular items for sale to foreigners. Each tribe is quite distinct and prefers to avoid intermarriage. Their foods and traditions are different as well.

The people live off the land, growing crops and bringing their handicrafts into the markets to earn money. They practice a form of agriculture called slash and burn. In between plantings, the land is cleared, set afire, then allowed to rest while the people move on to farm another piece of land. Unlike the rest of

Members of the Magh tribe

Bangladesh, this area is sparsely populated. However, it has been government policy for some time to move Bengalis to the Chittagong Hill Tracts where they can farm the land for themselves. So many Bengalis have been moved in that they are thought to number half of the total population of the area. By claiming the land, they make it impossible for the tribal people to live their seminomadic life, farming in different places. The tribes believe that the land is there for everyone to share. In addition, a great portion of the land was lost forever when it was flooded for a hydroelectric project in the 1960s.

In part because of the conflict between these different groups, the Chittagong Hill Tracts is considered off limits to outsiders without a special permit, and the permit is very rarely given.

Bihari children

THE BIHARIS

The tribal people living in the Chittagong Hill Tracts are one of the two groups of non-Bengali people living in Bangladesh. The other group is the Biharis, Muslims who were living in the state of Bihar in India at the time of Partition in 1947. Being Muslims, they fled India for East Pakistan, to live in a Muslim country. But they have always lived apart from the Bengalis, speaking Urdu, their own language, and practicing their own traditions.

When the war for independence began, the Biharis welcomed the arrival of the Pakistani army because they did not want Bangladesh to be an independent country; they wanted to remain part of Pakistan. The Biharis held many of the best jobs in Bangladesh, then called East Pakistan. When Bangladesh gained its independence, the Biharis lost everything. Their jobs were taken;

The Biharis would like to have enough money to move to Pakistan.

in many cases their homes were taken, and their lives were often in jeopardy. They were hated by the Bangladeshis for being sympathetic to West Pakistan. Many returned to Pakistan after the war, but there are still several hundred thousand who would like to go back but don't have the financial resources to do so. They are truly caught between two cultures, and will probably live out their lives as strangers in the land.

THE SUNDARBANS

While the Chittagong Hill Tracts have few people, the least populated area in Bangladesh is the Sundarbans—a mysterious mix of land and water where tigers roam, men fish, and country people enter the forest to cut wood for cooking fires. The Sundarbans are swampy forests that stretch along the Bay of

Left: A river in the Sundarbans   Right: A marabou stork

Bengal from the delta of the Meghna River in Bangladesh to the delta of the Houghly River in India. The amount of land in the Sundarbans is subject to the movement of the tides. On average, the tides rise and fall 12 feet (3.7 meters), twice a day. During the monsoons, the movement of water is even greater than that.

It is thought that the name *Sundarbans* comes from "forest of *sundari*," a Bengali term that describes the great mangroves—the largest stand of these trees found anywhere in the world.

The Sundarbans separate the plains of Bangladesh from the Bay of Bengal. The great stands of trees are laced with river channels that snake around, changing course frequently as storms sweep over the areas. The Sundarbans act as a buffer, shielding the rest of this low-lying countryside from some of the worst of the wind and tide.

The Sundarbans are rich in many kinds of plant and animal life. Crocodiles live in the many estuaries, growing to three times the size of a man. Pythons, which often reach 15 feet (4.6 meters) in

Some animals that live in the Sundarbans are the rhesus monkey (left), the monitor lizard (top left), the crocodile (top right), and the spotted deer (above).

length, thrive here as well. Among the many birds is the lesser marabou stork, a scavenger that feeds off animals killed by others. There is no fresh water available at all, but animals such as the rhesus monkeys drink the salt water with no ill effects. When the monkeys find fruit that has fallen off the trees into the mud, they carry it to a saltwater creek where they wash it off before eating it. Spotted deer sometimes stand up on their hind legs to eat leaves off the trees. The fierce-looking monitor lizard is found here, as are wild pigs. The pigs, like the monkeys, eat fruit too, but they don't bother to wash it off.

During the four-month-long fishing season, ten thousand fishermen take their boats out on the winding river channels and

Weighing fish (above) and nets used for fishing (right)

catch many species of fish. During the hot and humid months of
April and May, just before the cyclones form, the honey collectors
enter the forest. They go deep into the Sundarbans, far from shore,
looking for nests the bees create on the branches of the
mangroves. When they find one, they build a fire to smoke out the
bees. Then the men climb the trees and take the honeycomb, rich
in honey. The workers are often stung by the bees, but they feel
the reward is worth the pain. Honey from the Sundarbans is a
special treat.

TIGERS

The danger to everyone who enters the watery mangrove
swamps of the Sundarbans comes from the beautiful but fierce
royal Bengal tiger. Bengal tigers are found only in Asia, where
they once roamed over much of the southern and eastern portion

of the continent. Today they have a far more restricted range. Loss of habitat through hunting and timber harvesting has reduced the number of tigers drastically. In Bangladesh today, tigers are found principally in the Sundarbans. About four hundred to five hundred tigers are estimated to remain in the Sundarbans, which include areas in Bangladesh as well as in India to the west.

Male tigers live solitary lives except during the mating period. Tigresses and their cubs live together as a family until the cubs are old enough to hunt on their own. A tigress will usually have two or three cubs at one time.

Although wild animals normally do not attack people unless they are provoked or are too weak or old to hunt their usual pre the tigers in the Sundarbans regularly kill and eat people who cross their paths. They don't seem to differentiate between the spotted deer that are their natural prey and men.

Unlike many other big cats, tigers are great swimmers and are completely at home in the changeable land-and-water environment of the Sundarbans. Tigers have been seen swimming across even the broadest channels in the Sundarbans. They often catch their prey at water holes, chasing spotted deer right into the water.

But they also will attack men in the water, sometimes swimming out to the flimsy fishing boats and pulling a fisherman right off the boat. A man is hardly an opponent for a tiger who may weigh 500 pounds (227 kilograms) and stretch 12 feet (3.7 meters) from nose to tail. Tigers are the largest members of the cat family, much bigger than lions.

There is a theory that the tigers in the Sundarbans are so aggressive because of the salt water. But their willingness to attack people is a difficult problem to solve, because the tigers are

Bengal tigers in the Sundarbans are dangerous because they have attacked humans. It seems that they cannot tell the difference between men and their natural prey.

themselves an endangered species. Conservationists have looked for ways to keep the tigers from attacking people without resorting to shooting. They have tried two schemes that seem to be working.

FACE TO FACE

In areas where fishermen are often found, dummies that look remarkably like fishermen have been set up. When tigers approach, they touch a wire that gives them a mild electric shock. Another scheme, even simpler, seems to be working also. Honey hunters are almost always attacked from the rear as they walk through the forest seaching for beehives, so they have been given masks that look just like a face. They wear these on the backs of their heads. During the first three years after they were given the masks, not one man wearing a mask was killed by a tiger.

But authorities are worried that eventually the tigers will figure

Tigers are excellent swimmers.

out the difference between a dummy and a real man, and between a mask and a real face. Tigers are not only strong and fierce, they are very shrewd.

FORESTS

Except for the Chittagong Hill Tracts, the mangrove forests of the Sundarbans are among the last of the forests left in Bangladesh. The mangrove trees themselves are considered desirable for use both as timber and as firewood. In a country where most of the people cook over wood fires, cutting down trees for fuel has resulted in a drastic loss of woodlands. Nearly all of the trees that are cut down are used for firewood. While loss of forests elsewhere in Bangladesh means more flooding, in the Sundarbans it also weakens the barrier that the dense vegetation provides in the time of cyclones and tidal waves.

Chapter 6

BUSINESS AND

AGRICULTURE

RESOURCES

If you ask the Bangladeshis, "What is the great natural resource of your country?" they will probably answer, "People." It is true that the thing that Bangladesh has the most of is people. But apart from that, Bangladesh has a great deal of natural gas, the only natural resource in the country that has been harnessed and used for the good of the people. With the widespread distribution of natural gas—thirteen gas fields have been located so far— Bangladesh hopes to become completely self-sufficient in energy. This is truly a vital goal for a country whose people have such low incomes. The consumption of energy in Bangladesh is among the lowest in the world. Even with such a low level of consumption, however, Bangladesh still spends more than two-thirds of its export earnings on oil.

There are substantial reserves of coal that have not been worked. There are no major industries in the area where coal is found that would make it profitable to establish coal mines. There are unknown reserves of petroleum in Bangladesh and in the waters adjacent to it. A small amount of oil production has been started, and the oil is refined locally.

Although Bangladesh has good water resources, the terrain is not suitable for harnessing the rivers to create hydroelectric power. That would require dramatic drops of water, as in mountainous country, but Bangladesh is mostly flat land. There is one hydroelectric power station in the Chittagong Hills. But electricity isn't really a practical kind of energy in a country where most of the people live in the countryside, far from city life. Natural gas, used for cooking, is a much better alternative and could also take the place of wood. Because the amount of wood available in Bangladesh is diminishing rapidly, there will come a time when there will be no choice but to use natural gas.

BUSINESS AND INDUSTRY

In its short life as an independent nation, Bangladesh has had to create virtually an entire economy. Many of the policies of the British, who ruled until 1947, and the Pakistanis, who drained Bangladesh of resources until 1971, left the country with very little in the way of a manufacturing economy.

The business of most of Bangladesh is still agriculture, notably rice and jute, but new industries have grown in the past decade that take advantage of the country's excess supply of labor and its people's willingness to try something new and to work very hard to make a success of it.

SMALL LOANS

In every sense the economy of Bangladesh is a small-scale operation; but if you put together enough small businesses, you can wind up with a significant investment. This is the idea behind

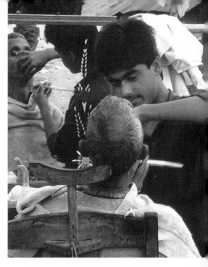

*Small businesses might include selling soap (far left) or bananas (middle),
cutting hair at the roadside (top right), or making pottery (right).*

the Grameen Bank, a local bank that specializes in the smallest of
loans. A woman (three-quarters of the borrowers are women)
may ask for $90 to buy a cow, or even less to start a business
selling mirrors and bananas, frying peanuts, or anything else that
will help make money for her family.

A woman who borrows money to buy a cow could earn money
to pay the loan by selling the cow's milk. With the money earned
the family might invest in a bicycle rickshaw, which the sons
could use to earn even more money. A whole family prospers
from this tiny loan.

The bank was started in 1979 by Mohammad Yunus, who
believed that women had the greatest incentive to raise their
families out of poverty. Traditional banks require some form of
security, but half the people in Bangladesh are landless and have
no security to offer. Yunus's faith has been justified: 98 percent of

the loans are repaid. The bank operates in more than fourteen thousand villages and, although the average loan is just $76, lends a total of $6 million a month.

GARMENT INDUSTRY

The biggest recent success story in Bangladesh has been the development of the garment industry. This industry is ideally suited to Bangladesh, which has an excess of labor. Garments may be made in small-scale operations by workers who are skilled with their hands but haven't much formal education. More than 300,000 people, most of them women, are employed in these companies. As they become responsible for supporting their families, many women also are finding it possible to direct their lives for the first time.

Traditionally, women in Bangladesh have been completely dependent on the men in their lives—first their fathers, then their husbands. With the chance to earn money for the first time in their lives, women now have the ability to be financially independent. This creates a new incentive to have fewer children, because competition for jobs is keen and women who are home with babies will lose out. The garment industry is also a way to make a living aside from agriculture, and with the increasing pressure on the land this is vitally important.

When Bangladesh began exporting finished garments in 1979, the industry earned $1 million in profits. Ten years later, it was $450 million. It's not surprising that Bangladesh says it has revolutionized the lives of women there. Bangladesh has become the fourth-largest supplier of cotton apparel to the United States. In the future, Bangladesh hopes to establish cotton mills to make

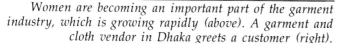

Women are becoming an important part of the garment industry, which is growing rapidly (above). A garment and cloth vendor in Dhaka greets a customer (right).

cloth; right now, all garments are made from imported fabrics. This would provide additional jobs for Bangladeshis and it would help the overall economy by reducing the amount of foreign exchange needed to purchase cloth.

LEATHER

On a smaller scale is the new leather finishing industry in Chittagong and Khulna, using hides from cattle and goats. Although they generate less income than the garment industry, the leather finishing companies have shown remarkable growth in just a few years. The industry accounts for earnings as high as $90 million a year. The quality of the skins is rated very favorably in the international marketplace.

BREAKING SHIPS

One of the most unusual occupations in Bangladesh, or anywhere in the world, is that of ship breaking. There comes a time in the life of a ship—even the biggest ocean liners or freighters—when it has outlived its usefulness. But what do you do with such a ship? You can't park it in a lot and forget about it. And there is recyclable metal and equipment on a ship, even one that is too old to sail anymore. The answer is to break it up. And one of the few places on earth where this is done is in Bangladesh.

From the far corners of the earth, shipowners send ships on their last journey to the port of Chittagong. Here, brokers bid on the ships. The one who offers the most money for what is going to be a huge pile of scrap gets the job. It can cost $3.5 million to buy a ship that is going to be torn apart.

As the ship comes into port, the broker directs the captain to do what a sailor tries hard *not* to do—to steer the ship up onto the beach. This makes it easier for the men to get to work; and in a situation where there is virtually no electrical equipment to make the job easier, any advantage is eagerly sought.

Torches are used to cut flat sections of steel. Otherwise, the men simply rely on sledge hammers and their strength to take the ship apart, right down to the last bolt and screw. Each part is then sold, either for scrap or to reuse. Much of the metal goes into the smelter at Chittagong, to be melted down and used to make something entirely new. The metal from the broken ships is the greatest source of steel in Bangladesh.

Like ants, the men scramble over the ships. In just eight weeks, they can reduce a huge ocean liner to metal sheets. Their wages are very, very low, but they welcome the jobs. There are few jobs

Farm women tend cows and crops.

in Bangladesh, even for people who have far more education than most of these men.

Ship breaking may have been inspired by misfortune: in the late 1960s a ship ran aground in Chittagong during a storm and a smart businessman bought it for scrap and then had it broken up. Although the industry didn't develop immediately, the idea was planted.

RICE

In Bangladesh more people live on each acre of land than almost anywhere else in the world. This causes severe problems because most Bangladeshis earn their living from farming, and there is not enough farmland available. Farmers have small areas to grow crops, and not enough food is grown to feed the population. Rice is the principal crop grown for personal consumption; it is eaten every day, and provides about 90 percent

Above: A rice paddy in the Chittagong Hill Tracts
Right: Rice merchants

of the calories consumed each day. But the amount of rice grown on each acre of land in Bangladesh is one of the lowest in the world. The plots that are worked by Bangladesh peasants are too small to allow the use of efficient machinery. Some of the land is worked with a plow pulled by an ox, or in some cases the farmers just use a pointed stick to dig holes for the seeds. Planting is done in the wet season and is planned to take advantage of the monsoon rains. The right amount of rain enables the rice to grow and be ready for harvesting by December and January. This primary rice-growing period is called *aghani*, the winter harvest. In the spring, known as the *rabi* harvest, crops of various vegetables may be planted. In the summer, the *kharif* crops are planted, including maize (corn), millet, and a second crop of rice.

Although Bangladesh gets a tremendous amount of rain, it is undependable and often falls in a short period, causing flooding. To make better use of the rainwater and to increase the amount of rice grown, a major effort is under way, supported by the

A breakfast of chappatis *and curry and tea*

Bangladesh government, to bring more of the land under irrigation. (The more control farmers have over the water available to them, the more they can produce. Irrigation also permits farmers to grow a second crop of rice each year, during the "dry" season.) Each year thousands of pumps are installed to bring water to farmland. During the monsoon season, farmers can plant the tiny seedlings while the rain is pouring down on them.

Bangladesh now grows about 90 percent of the rice it uses each year. The amount of rice grown also has been increasing through the use of fertilizers and pesticides. Thus, as the population grows, so does rice production.

Wheat also is grown in Bangladesh, in the southern part of the country where there is not as much rainfall. People who live in the cities gradually are adding more wheat to their diets in place of rice. The wheat is used to make *chappatis*, flat disks of bread, that form the base for whatever else the person has to eat: butter, vegetables, or a curry. Wheat grows faster than rice, and is less

Everyone helps in the peeling of potatoes for a marriage feast.

expensive to grow. After the wheat is harvested, during the dry winter months, other crops can be planted on the same land until the next wheat crop is planted the following year.

LANDLESS

As a farmer's children grow up and marry and need their own land to work, the farmer divides his land among his children. Over the years the size of the average farm has grown smaller and smaller; today, it is about 2 acres (0.8 hectare). But many families have even smaller farms than that. A farm as small as 1 acre (0.4 hectare) isn't big enough to feed even one family. More than six million families have less than a half acre of land.

Many farmers don't own any land at all. Many have had to sell their land to buy food; in many cases there simply wasn't any land left to be divided for the next generation. More than half the rural families in Bangladesh don't own land. About one-fourth of the land is owned by 5 percent of the families, and many farmers work on land owned by others. Although fewer people own their own farmland with each passing generation, the number of people who depend upon agriculture for their livelihood continues to grow. However, there are other developing industries that provide work for many of these landless Bangladeshis.

JUTE

While rice is the most important food crop grown in Bangladesh, jute is the most important cash crop. Because 75 percent of all the money Bangladesh earns through exports comes from selling jute, it is often called the "golden" crop.

Jute grows in the form of very slender shoots, each one no bigger than a finger in diameter. It grows straight up, all the plants crowding close together, reaching as high as 15 feet (4.6 meters). The stalks are bare at the bottom but covered with many leaves along the top half. The climate in northwest and central Bangladesh, especially along the major rivers, is ideally suited for jute.

Jute requires a great deal of labor, the one commodity Bangladesh has in abundance, and it provides farmers with a way to earn money. Because wages in Bangladesh are lower than in other countries that produce jute, Bangladesh has become the largest jute producer in the world. When the jute is harvested, the workers tie bundles of the slender stalks together and leave them in the field until the leaves shed. Then the stalks are soaked for as long as a month until they soften and the fiber can be stripped from the plants. The workers stand in water up to their waists while they strip the stalks. After the stripping, the fibers are washed and draped over poles or lines to dry in the sun. Once

A boat loaded with jute

they are ready to be processed, the fibers are tied into huge bundles that are carried to boats that float them downstream to the waiting mills.

In the mills, dotted around the country, the jute is spun into threads that can be woven into a variety of fabrics. These mills create additional opportunities to make money from the growth of jute. Jute is used principally for rope and twine, for carpet backing and carpeting, and for industrial quality sacks used for flour, wheat, and many other agricultural products. In Bangladesh, mills to convert the raw jute into these products may be found in many cities, including Jessore, Shaka, Chandpur, and the port of Chittagong. The United States has traditionally been the biggest purchaser of jute products from Bangladesh. When the United States supplies food to foreign countries, it is often asked to use jute bags because additional uses can be found for the empty bags.

TEA

Bangladesh is a tea-drinking country that grows its own tea in the extreme northeastern part of the country, known as Sylhet Hills, as well as in sections of Chittagong. About 100,000 people are employed in the tea industry. With so many other countries growing tea, Bangladesh is able to sell its tea only to Pakistan and at not very high prices. Most of the crop, however, is consumed by the Bangladeshis.

FISHERIES

Fishing is a natural occupation for people in a land that has as much water as Bangladesh. About three-fourths of the people who live in the countryside fish for food during the flood season. An important commercial fish industry has been developed in the Bay of Bengal in the areas of Cox's Bazar and Khulna.

Fisheries that specialize in shrimp and frog legs have increased their earnings enormously since the industry began in 1977. Fisheries are actively involved in raising shrimp and exercising control over the product. Fresh and frozen seafood has quickly moved into second place in exports, surpassed only by jute. Japan buys more than half of Bangladesh's seafood exports.

Chapter 7

THE WAY OF LIFE

COUNTRY BOATS

The landscape of Bangladesh is laced with waterways, making travel by boat the simplest and most logical way to travel within the country. Small boats, poled or paddled by hand, carry people and goods across the many little rivers.

These small boats are called country boats because they ply the waters in areas that are far from Bangladesh's few cities. Country boats are used to carry jute to the mills. People travel from village to village by boat or from their villages to the market. They use the boats in places where it is impossible to build bridges or where bridges have been washed out by floods. There isn't enough money in the country's budget to build bridges at all the crossing points where they're needed. In many cases, the country can't afford to build bridges strong enough to withstand the violent rainstorms and floods that so often hit Bangladesh. During the rainy season travel by boat is the only way to get around in Bangladesh.

Opposite page: A port on the Padma River at Dhaka
Inset: Boats on a small canal at Maulvi Bazar

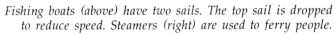
Fishing boats (above) have two sails. The top sail is dropped to reduce speed. Steamers (right) are used to ferry people.

When they go upstream, against the current, the boatmen must use their muscle power to move through the water. When they travel with the current, they often raise a sail and take advantage of the wind, making their jobs much easier. This also makes the trip much faster.

The country boat is such a familiar sight in Bangladesh that it is the symbol of one of the major political parties, the Awami League. There are about 300,000 country boats in the country, some of them big enough to carry up to 35 tons (31,752 kilograms) of cargo with just the use of manpower and sometimes a sail. These simple boats ride very low in the water, especially when they're loaded with freight.

Much larger boats, including steamers and barges, are used for longer trips and for carrying heavier loads. Millions of tons of cargo are moved about on the inland waterways—there are more than 4,971 miles (8,000 kilometers) of navigable waterways in Bangladesh. The steamers are overcrowded and often one of them capsizes, causing many people to drown. There are too many people trying to get to their destinations and too few boats to take them there. Oceangoing boats form the rest of Bangladesh's water fleet. They operate at the major ports including Chittagong and Chalna, both on the Bay of Bengal.

Roads are of secondary importance in Bangladesh, in part because they are so difficult to maintain in a country where flooding is so common but also because the cost of fuel is high. it is estimated that there are about 6,835 miles (11,000 kilometers) of roads suitable for vehicles, but only half are paved. Frequently, vehicles traveling on roads must be transferred to ferries to get across the many rivers, both large and small, that cut across the roads.

BICYCLE RICKSHAWS

In the cities, bicycle rickshaws are still the way most people get around. A rickshaw is little more than a seat on wheels with a covering of woven jute or fabric to protect the passenger—all attached to the front end of a bicycle. The driver sits on the bicycle seat, or stands up, and pedals the passenger around town. It's extremely hard work to pedal a rickshaw, and many of the drivers have to work for ten or twelve hours a day. They barely earn enough money to buy necessities. But for men who have migrated to the cities and are unable to do any other kind of work, it's better than no job at all.

Rickshaws are supposed to be registered, and it is believed that there are more than 180,000 of them throughout the country. Each one is usually used for two shifts, giving more men employment. The rickshaw serves people in place of taxis or private cars, which

The rickshaw (left) is used as a taxi. The buses (middle) are sometimes a little crowded. A train station (right) in Dhaka isn't very busy

would be much too expensive for most people. The rickshaw doesn't depend on gasoline either—it's a pollution-free form of transportation.

There are some trains in Bangladesh, with about 1,740 miles (2,800 kilometers) of track; but both the number of locomotives and the amount of freight carried by trains have declined in the past decade. Most of the lines run north and south, following the direction of the rivers. It's difficult to build rail lines with so many waterways to cross.

It's a matter of pride for Bangladesh, as for many of the poorer nations in the world, that it has its own national airline, Biman Bangladesh Airlines. The airline provides service inside the country as well as to a number of other countries. There are four airports in Bangladesh that can handle large jet aircraft.

*Left: The Old High Court building,
or Curzon Hall, was built by the
British in the early part of the
twentieth century. Above: a* bangla,
from which we get the word "bungalow"

CITIES

The cities of Bangladesh teem with people. Each year they grow
more crowded as people who have lost their land through natural
disasters or for other reasons arrive from the countryside. Since
the main cities date from ancient times, the history of the area is
preserved in the buildings. The Mughal influence is seen in the
onion-shaped roofs, elegant arches, and lovely symmetry. When
the British arrived in the nineteenth century, they brought their
Victorian architecture, layering it right on top of the Mughal style.
Often, these buildings were an imitation of those in England, and
were not at all suitable for the very different climate. Finally,
modern buildings were added to the mix.

We have the Bengalis to thank for the concept of the
bungalow—a word that comes from the Bengali word *bangla*,
meaning "living quarters."

Above: Old Dhaka is a crowded, busy, interesting section of the capital.
Below: The University of Dhaka (left) and the tomb of Bibi Hari (right)

A modern section of Dhaka

DHAKA

The capital of Bangladesh is also a provincial capital. It has served an administrative role for four hundred years, as various rulers controlled the region. But the city has existed in one form or another for much longer. When the British ruled Bengal, the name of the city was spelled "Dacca." After Bangladesh became independent, the spelling was changed to "Dhaka." Today, Dhaka, the country's largest city, has a population of about 4.5 million people—more people per square mile than almost any other city in the world. (Only Lagos, Nigeria, is more densely populated.) Dhaka is a major river port for Bangladesh, and most of the goods coming into the city arrive via country boats.

One of Dhaka's best-known sights is the Shahid Minar, a monument to those who died in the language riots of 1952, located near Shaka Medical College Hospital. Dhaka also is known for the unfinished Lalbagh Fort, built in the 1600s. The daughter of Prince Mohammad Azam, Bibi Hari, died while the fort was being constructed. Construction was stopped and a tomb was built for the daughter. Dhaka is sometimes called the City of Mosques and is also home to the University of Dhaka, which dates from 1921. The city has many open-air markets where farmers bring their produce to sell directly to the city dwellers.

The beach of Cox's Bazar and Chittagong (inset)

CHITTAGONG AND OTHER PLACES

Among the sights in Chittagong is a museum of ethnology, appropriately located here, where the largest gathering of non-Bengalis lives.

Cox's Bazar, a sea resort about 100 miles (161 kilometers) south of Chittagong, has one of the longest sea beaches in the world. The beach, which is very broad, seems to stretch endlessly, as far as one can see, along the Bay of Bengal. In addition to the beach, Cox's Bazar is known for its many pagodas and Buddhist shrines. The town was named after British Captain Hiram Cox, who settled the region with immigrants from Burma in 1798.

Khulna is where many of Bangladesh's Hindus live. It is a major river port.

A new hospital in Dhaka

HEALTH

In many areas of health and health care, Bangladesh ranks quite low among all the countries of the world. The infant mortality rate, a basic measure of the health of a nation, is very high; one of every five children born will die by the age of five. Fewer than 10 percent of the children are immunized against childhood diseases, so preventable diseases such as measles, tetanus, and pertussis (whooping cough) rank very high in the cause of childhood deaths. The average life expectancy is about fifty years.

Many health problems are connected with the other major issues facing Bangladesh today. Flooding often brings with it a breakdown in sanitation and the spread of infectious diseases. A lack of pure drinking water allows communicable diseases to spread. Typical of poor nations, Bangladesh struggles with such basic problems as diarrhea and malnutrition. With its tropical climate, Bangladesh is also home to malaria, a disease spread by mosquitoes. When illness or disease strikes there are few doctors to turn to, especially in rural areas.

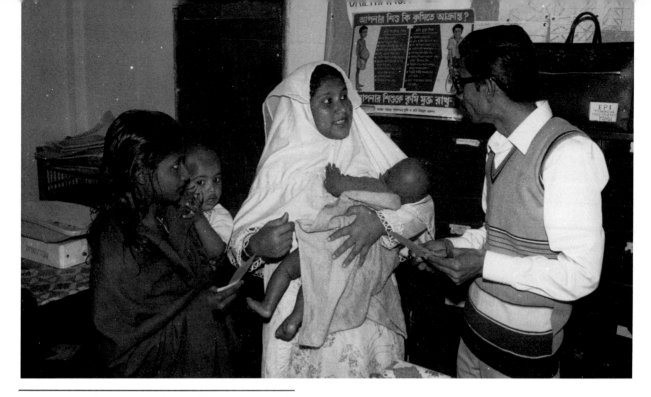

A mother and her children at a clinic

The greatest success Bangladesh has had in improving the lives of its people is the dramatic reduction in the birth rate. The population is growing at a rate of about 2.5 percent a year, down from a high of about 3.4 percent. Most of this decline occurred between 1961 and 1981. Bangladeshis say simply, ''We had to reduce the birth rate; there was no choice.'' But it is much simpler to say than to do in a culture where children are needed to work and where a woman's value is still measured by her ability to bear children. The nation's family planning goals have been only about half as successful as had been hoped.

EDUCATION

Because the Bengali culture has such a rich literary tradition, education is highly prized. Unfortunately, it is difficult for all but a few to get more than a basic education, and the literacy rate is

An elementary school classroom

only 20 percent. That figure only tells part of the story: the rate for boys is twice that for girls. In the countryside, it is extremely difficult to get an education. There aren't enough schools to accommodate all the children who want to attend, and there isn't transportation to get them to the schools. School attendance is not required, although most villages have some type of elementary school. Children in cities have a much better chance of going to and staying in school. As a result, the literacy rate in the cities is about twice that in the rural areas. For children who only attend primary schools, the ability to read and write is often lost as they grow older, for they have little or no chance to use these skills.

Although an estimated 44 million students were in primary schools in the mid-1980s, fewer than 3 million went on to secondary schools. Going farther up the educational ladder, there were about 600,000 college students during the same period. The relatively high number of college students compared with

Above: A class of girls reciting their lesson
Right: A private school in Barisal

secondary school students is an indication that students who make it through the high school level are expected to go on to college. A high school education is not a goal by itself in Bangladesh.

CHOOSING A LANGUAGE

One of the problems the education system had to deal with immediately after independence was the decision to use Bengali instead of English as the language of instruction. This took time because all textbooks had to be translated into Bengali. The result, in two decades, has been a decline in the use of English in Bangladesh. While this gives the Bangladeshis pride in their own language and culture, it puts more distance between them and the rest of the world. When English was more widely spoken, chances for employment outside the country were better and textbooks were more widely available.

Students at the University of Dhaka

In major cities such as Dhaka, parents with school-age children can choose between schools where either Bengali or English is the language of instruction. Those who choose the English-language school are generally people whose income is well above the average. They expect their children to become part of the business and technical world outside Bangladesh, where a knowledge of English is vital to their success.

Children from Bangladesh's national cultural troupe who visited the United States in 1990 as part of the World Summit for Children are examples of this language division. The girls were unusually well educated. Most of the children attended English-speaking schools in Dhaka, although one, who went to a Bengali-speaking school, also spoke English very well. Part of their ability to speak English well, they said, was because so many programs on television were American programs, so they heard American English spoken often. Their curriculum includes math, science, Islamic history, English, and Bengali; they begin to study English right from the beginning.

Top: The air force drops relief goods to flood victims of the 1991 cyclone. Left: People reach for food being distributed from a bus.

Chapter 8

BANGLADESH

AND THE WORLD

Bangladesh has commanded a high degree of attention from the nations of the world since its struggle for independence began and through the years that followed. Much of the attention has focused on the country's constant need for aid and its frequent natural disasters. It often seems to the outside world that it cannot be possible for the land, or the nation, to survive because of all the problems it must face. But the people don't have a choice; they must survive, and to do so, they continue to seek and receive help from the rest of the world.

FOREIGN AID

The struggles of the people of Bangladesh have touched the hearts of people, and the treasuries of governments, all over the world. Since its independence, foreign aid has often made the difference in the nation's survival. In the first year after independence, agencies such as Save the Children, others coming directly from foreign governments, and UNICEF were working in Bangladesh.

While food was the principal form of aid in the country's first years, that has begun to decrease. In its place is aid of more long-term value: equipment to help the people increase their own food production and water supplies. Unfortunately, the country has such a poor record in self-government that it has not been able to absorb and make use of all the funds available to it. The World Bank has been the overseer of aid to Bangladesh, coordinating the efforts and donations of the various government agencies and other contributing institutions through the Bangladesh Aid Group, which was created in 1974.

The United States gave the greatest amount of aid for most of the years that followed Bangladesh's independence until the 1980s, when Japan became a donor of equal measure.

As with so many other areas of life in Bangladesh, the constantly growing population has made it difficult for the country to get ahead in providing for the needs of its people. This combined with a lack of governmental organization, governmental corruption, and the genuine physical difficulties that the land and the climate create, has left Bangladesh with an ongoing need for aid.

The new government of Begum Khaleda Zia is faced with the task of solving the problem that accounts for Bangladesh's unstable political history: the many factions in Bangladesh that must be satisfied before any government can even begin to govern.

WAR IN THE GULF

At the time of Iraq's takeover of Kuwait in the autumn of 1990, more than 100,000 Bangladeshis were working in those two countries. Although Iraq is a Muslim nation like Bangladesh, that common bond was of little help to the Bangladeshis, who were all

In 1990, Bangladeshi refugees stayed at this camp on the Iraqi-Turkey border until their own country was able to bring them home.

dismissed from their jobs. However, unlike many of the other nations of the world whose people were working in the gulf countries, Bangladesh could not afford to send airplanes immediately to bring its people home. Many had to wait in refugee camps in the desert, not knowing when they would be able to return to their own country. The upheaval cost the government of Bangladesh an estimated one billion dollars overall, counting the loss of income from the workers as well as the cost of resettlement.

The long-term costs of all this to Bangladesh are expected to be even greater. While many unskilled laborers were involved, there were also many engineers and doctors who had gone to the gulf region to work because Bangladesh could not offer them employment. These workers regularly sent money to their relatives at home. It is estimated that each Bangladeshi working abroad supported as many as twelve people at home. This money was spent at small businesses in villages and towns all over the country, and so the people who owned those businesses came to count on that income, too. Finally, relatives often were able to arrange better marriages because families felt they could rely on the money coming from overseas.

Some Bangladeshi soldiers, about three thousand of them, were sent to the region as a peace-keeping force before the war actually began. They were sent by the government of Bangladesh, according to then-President Ershad, to help defend the holy sites of Islam. They wound up at the front, fighting alongside the multinational forces.

The war in the Persian Gulf disrupted the lives and financial security of hundreds of thousands of people in Bangladesh.

FARMING SUFFERS

The Gulf War affected Bangladesh indirectly, as well. Because of a shortage of diesel fuel, many of the pumps used for irrigation in Bangladesh were not in service. As a result many farmers lost their winter crop. There is another concern about the long-term effects of this war. Almost all of Kuwait's oil wells were set on fire by the Iraqi armies before they were forced out of Kuwait. The hundreds of oil-fed fires were sending huge clouds of greasy black smoke into the air. Some scientists are afraid that the smoke will eventually make its way over South Asia and that it will change the normal pattern of monsoon rains. Should that occur, then Bangladesh's entire rice crop could be in jeopardy.

BANGLADESH AND THE UNITED STATES

The United States was an ally of Pakistan in 1971 when Bangladesh became independent. The United States policy was based on the many conflicting needs and desires of the major powers in the region, especially China and India. For example, when India backed East Pakistan's desire to be independent, India did so in large part because it was forced to take in millions of refugees fleeing the war. Because the United States and East Pakistan found themselves on opposite sides during the war for independence, relations between Bangladesh and the United States were very poor during the country's first years as a nation. However, they slowly improved toward the end of the 1970s. A decade later, the United States-Bangladesh relationship had changed dramatically.

Even though the United States has been a significant aid giver during the past two decades, Bangladesh does not have a particular closeness with the United States. As a Muslim country, Bangladesh naturally inclines more toward other Muslim nations. This was made clear during the Gulf War. Although some three thousand Bangladeshi soldiers were fighting on the side of the allies, a half million Bangladeshis in Dhaka were demonstrating *against* the war because it was a war against their fellow Muslims. The bonds of religion came in conflict with loyalty to the nation, and many directed their protest specifically against the United States, which had a leading role in the war against Iraq.

During the Cold War Bangladesh considered itself a nonaligned nation, siding with neither the democratic nor the Communist governments. With the collapse of the former Soviet Union and its allies, relations have improved between the United States and Bangladesh. After Bangladesh's help in the Gulf War and following their 1991 elections, the U.S. showed its approval in a very substantial way: it wrote off $300 million of Bangladesh's debt.

INDIA: POWERFUL NEIGHBOR

India, Bangladesh's nearest and biggest neighbor, is more of a cause for daily concern than the United States. When Pakistan was created, millions of people from the newly independent nations of India and Pakistan were uprooted. Because Bangladesh was then part of Pakistan, relations with India were hostile. This situation changed dramatically when India came to the aid of East Pakistan in its struggle against West Pakistan in 1971. India was the decisive element in Bangladesh's war against West Pakistan and in its ultimate independence. This was a difficult position for India, a Hindu nation taking up a cause on behalf of a Muslim nation. The need to settle the millions of refugees caught in the war forced India's government to overlook the religious dilemma. At the same time, there were many Hindus living in East Pakistan whose lives were in special peril as the new Muslim nation was being created.

Through the years, the instability of Bangladesh's government and the series of violent changes of government has led to fears that India would step in simply to have a more stable neighbor on its very long eastern border. Indeed, parts of India are actually wrapped around Bangladesh, creating a kind of embrace that is nearly all-encompassing. Except for a tiny section where Bangladesh borders Burma and along the Bay of Bengal, the two countries share hundreds of miles of common borders.

Although political and religious differences are at the heart of some of the disagreements between the two countries, Bangladesh has continually been frustrated by India's refusal to cooperate on matters pertaining to control of the waterways that lead from India into Bangladesh. India has acted on its own through the years, building dams and diverting rivers entirely according to its own needs, with no thought to the consequences downriver in Bangladesh.

Movements of people between India and Bangladesh have occurred as a result of factional and tribal fights. Bangladeshis have moved across the border into India in search of work and land, both of which are in short supply at home. But with its own population of 850 million people, India has had to stop most Bangladesh immigration.

PAKISTAN: OLD ENEMY, NEW FRIEND

Through the years, as one of the two wings of Pakistan, the Bangladeshis had constantly been cheated out of their rightful share of the country's finances and had been pushed into a cycle of poverty. Then, during the fight for independence, West Pakistan had been brutal in its attack on the people of Bangladesh and had literally killed off the nation's intellectual core. After Bangladesh gained its independence from West Pakistan, the two were bitter enemies.

In time, the two nations began to move closer together in their political relations, and Pakistan formally recognized Bangladesh in 1974. With India, a huge Hindu presence standing between them, the two found that their common Muslim heritage gave them an important link after all. Bangladesh found common ground as well in its support of Pakistan's stand against the Soviet Union's war in Afghanistan, Pakistan's northern neighbor. The countries also had a common need to resettle Pakistanis who had been stranded in Bangladesh at the time of independence and who still wanted to return to Pakistan.

OTHER ASSOCIATIONS

Bangladesh was instrumental in the creation of SAARC—the South Asian Association for Regional Cooperation—an organization that also includes Bhutan, India, the Maldives, Nepal, Pakistan, and Sri Lanka. SAARC recognizes the unique needs of these countries and works toward cooperation in economic, technical, and cultural areas.

Relations between Bangladesh and the Arab states have grown closer through the years, a reflection of their common Muslim heritage. As the oil-rich Arab countries have grown in importance financially, they have given aid, mostly in the form of loans for Islamic education and culture. In return, the Bangladeshis formed one of the largest groups of foreigners working in the gulf states, up to the time of Iraq's invasion of Kuwait.

In 1974, Bangladesh was admitted to the United Nations and served a two-year term on the Security Council starting in 1978. In 1987, then-President Ershad received the United Nations' Population Award in recognition of the tremendous strides made by Bangladesh in reducing its birth rate.

BANGLADESHIS ABROAD

The largest community of Bangladeshis outside the country is in England. Although there were about one million Bangladeshis

Left: A Bangladeshi garment worker in London
Right: Indian and Bangladeshi restaurants in New York City

living and working abroad at one time, that number was reduced considerably by the Gulf War. The Bangladeshi community in England, centered in London, is a permanent one; these are families who have come looking for a better life. Many have become workers in Bangladeshi restaurants. They bring their Muslim religion to England as the core of their life. The relationship of colonizer and colonial has now come full circle.

Once it was the British who traveled to distant lands and conquered the people, imposing their culture. Now it is the foreigners who have come to England and brought with them the full force of their culture. In either case, the two cultures remain separate, coexisting but not merging.

ELECTIONS

In December 1990, Bangladesh's president, General Hussain Muhammad Ershad, was arrested and charged with illegal possession of firearms and with corruption. He was removed from his position as president and sentenced to ten years in jail.

In the following months, elections were held that proved to be the first truly democratic elections since Bangladesh became a nation. The two leading contenders for the top office were women: one, Begum Khaleda Zia was the widow of a former president of Bangladesh who had been assassinated in 1981. The other, Sheikh Hasina Wajed, was the daughter of Bangladesh's first leader, Sheikh Mujibur Rahman, who was also assassinated, in 1975. The ultimate, and surprising, winner was Khaleda Zia. Begum Khaleda is just one of a series of women who have come to power in the Indian subcontinent, but her position as head of government is still a rare one for a woman to hold anywhere in the world. Soon after her election, she was put to a terrible test of her ability to lead the nation.

CYCLONE OF 1991

On April 30, 1991, the worst cyclone since Bangladesh became a nation in 1971 swept up from the Bay of Bengal, devastating the coastline. Although the number of dead was officially set at 139,000, the cyclone directly affected the lives of ten million people. It was estimated that nearly a million homes had been destroyed, and tens of thousands of farm animals died in the violent storm. Those who were fortunate enough to reach some of the storm shelters along the coast were saved, although many of them lost what little they had in the way of possessions. The storm surge, a wall of water whipped by the wind, rose to twenty feet (six meters), submerging much of the southeastern coastal area of the country. Chittagong, the nation's major port, was severely damaged; sunken ships clogged the harbor.

Bangladeshi children cheered when United States marines brought relief to Sandwip Island.

The reaction of the world community was one of shock, and then the aid agencies set to work. The most immediate need was for shelter, food, and safe drinking water. The damage to the port of Chittagong prevented relief supplies from coming in by sea. When help did come, many in Bangladesh felt that the response was too little—and too slow. Newspaper articles asked the question on many people's minds: will it ever be possible to make progress in Bangladesh or will there always be another disaster to deal with? The Bangladeshis didn't have much time to think about these questions. They were too busy trying to survive and to start all over again.

The United States government responded in a novel way by sending a disaster relief force made up of nearly eight thousand military personnel. These men and women were actually on their way home from the Persian Gulf when they were diverted to Bangladesh. They arrived on navy ships and immediately set about giving direct assistance. Their mission focused on the need for food, clean water, and temporary shelter. The mission was called "Operation Sea Angel." The Bangladeshis named the soldiers "Angels of Mercy."

Marilyn Quayle, wife of the United States vice-president, visited Bangladesh a few weeks after the cyclone hit. When she arrived at Sandwip Island—off the coast of Bangladesh—which had been flattened by the hurricane, a man with his children at his side came up to her and said, "I'm sorry I don't have any flowers to give you." Mrs. Quayle replied, "You have your flowers in your children, these children which are alive." Mrs. Quayle was tremendously moved by the resiliency of the people and their determination to start over. During her three-day visit, she pitched in to help with the preparation of oral rehydration salts used in the treatment of diseases caused by dirty drinking water. The American soldiers left Bangladesh on May 24, but the need for aid of all kinds continued.

Although the cyclone of 1991 was an extreme example of the kinds of natural calamities that affect Bangladesh, it demonstrated that massive economic assistance could have an impact on Bangladesh's basic problems. For example, the storm shelters that had been built along the coast saved the lives of thousands of people, but only sixty-three shelters had been built, although five hundred were planned after the last major cyclone in 1985.

Finding funds to provide such basic needs as shelter, clean drinking water, and food to replace the crops lost in the storm was the major task facing Bangladesh's government, headed by Prime Minister Khaleda Zia.

Disasters focus the world's eyes on a country such as Bangladesh for a moment, but when the drama is over the basic

facts remain. A quarter of a million children under the age of five die *each year* in Bangladesh from dysentery, a severe form of diarrhea. That is more than all the people who died in the cyclone. Dysentery is a disease caused by bad drinking water. Bangladesh is a country with unusual burdens and few resources other than the incredible resilience of its people. That seems to be the real answer to the question: what is the future of Bangladesh?

The people have a better chance at holding on to their democratic system, and perhaps to reduce the corruption that has often seen their few resources diverted from the area with the greatest need. The change comes from the new form of government that was approved by the voters in September of 1991. Bangladesh is once again run under the parliamentary system. The strong presidency and one-party state that prevailed in 1975 under Sheikh Mujibur Rahman, and continued under a series of rulers thereafter, is finished. The government should be more responsive to the needs of the people. As it passed its twentieth year as an independent country, Bangladesh seemed to be maturing into a responsible member of the world community.

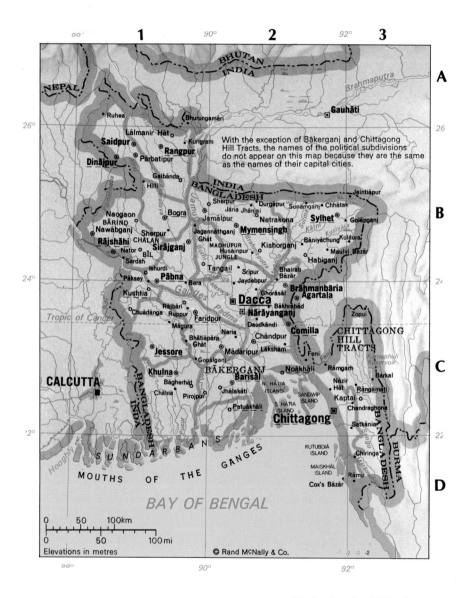

1 **2** **3**

BHUTAN
INDIA

NEPAL

A

26° • Ruhea • Bhurungamāri ⊡ **Gauhāti** 26

Saidpur Lālmanir Hāt • Kurigram With the exception of Bākerganj and Chittagong
Hill Tracts, the names of the political subdivisions
do not appear on this map because they are the same
as the names of their capital cities.

• **Rangpur** • Pārbatipur

Dinājpur

• Gaibānda

• Hilli INDIA
BANGLADESH • Jaintiāpur

• Sherpur • Durgāpur • Sunāmganj • Chhatak

Naogaon • Jāria Jhānjai **Sylhet** ° B
BĀRIND • **Bogra** • Jamālpur Netrakona • Golāpganj
Nawābganj Sherpur Jagannāthganj **Mymensingh** • Bāniyāchung • Kulāura•
Rājshāhi CHĀLAN Ghāt • Kishorganj • Maulvi Bāzār
• Nator BIL • **Sirājganj** MADHUPUR Husainpur • **Habiganj**
• Sardah JUNGLE
• Ishurdi • **Tangail** • Sripur Bhairab
• Pāksey **Pābna** • Jaydebpur Bāzār •
24° Kushtia • • Bera • Ghorāsāl **Brāhmanbāria** 24
• Rājbāri Ganges **Dacca** ⊡ **Agartala**
Chuādānga • Ruppur **Nārāyanganj** Bākhrābād • • Zopui
Tropic of Cancer • **Faridpur** Padma • Daudkāndi **CHITTAGONG**
• Māgura • Naria **Chāndpur** **Comilla** • **HILL**
Bhātiāpāra • Mādāripur • Lākshām • Feni **TRACTS**
• **Jessore** Ghāt Karnaphuli
• Gopālganj • **Noākhāli** • Rāmgarh Reservoir
C
Khulna • **BĀKERGANJ** • Nāzir • Barkal
CALCUTTA ■ • Bāgherhāt **Barisāl** N. HĀTIA Hāt • Rāngāmati
BANGLADESH • Chālna Pirojpur ISLAND **Kaptai**
INDIA • Jhālakāti SANDWIP • Chandraghona
• Patuākhāli S. HĀTIA ISLAND • Satkānia
ISLAND **Chittagong**
22° SUNDARBANS MOUTHS OF THE GANGES KUTUBDIĀ 22
Hooghly ISLAND • Chiringa
MAISKHĀL • Rāmu
MOUTHS OF THE GANGES ISLAND
Cox's Bāzār D

BAY OF BENGAL

0   50   100km
0   50   100mi
Elevations in metres © Rand McNally & Co.
-2 -2 -2

Map from Encyclopedia Britannica
© 1992 by Rand McNally, R.L. 92-S-85

MAP KEY

Atrai (river)	B2	Ghorasal	C2	Nazir Hat	C2
Bakerganj (region)	C2	Golapganj	B2	Netrakona	B2
Bakhrabad	C2	Gopalganj	C1	Noakhali	C2
Bangherhat	C1	Habiqanj	B2	North Hatia Island	C2
Baniyachung	B2	Hilli	B1	Pabna	B1
Barind (region)	B1	Husainpur	B2	Padma, see Ganges	
Barisal	C2	Ishurdi	B1	Paksey	B1
Barkal	C3	Jagannathganj Ghat	B1	Parbatipur	B1
Bengal, Bay of	D1, D2, D3	Jaintiapur	B3	Patuakhali	C2
Bera	C1	Jamalpur	B1	Pirojpur	C1
Bhairab Bazar	B2	Jamuna (river)	B1	Purnabhaba (river)	B1
Bhatiapara Ghat	C1	Jaria Jharjai	B2	Pusar (river)	C2
Bhurungamari	A1	Jaydebpur	C2	Rajbari	C1
Bogra	B1	Jessore	C1	Rajshahi	B1
Brahmanbaria	C2	Jhalakati	C2	Ramgarh	C2
Brahmaputra (river)	B2	Kalni (river)	B2	Ramu	D3
Burhi Ganga (river)	B1, B2	Kaptai	C3	Rangamati	C3
Chalan Bil (wetland)	B1	Karatoya (river)	B1	Rangpur	B1
Chalna	C1	Karnaphuli Reservoir	C3	Ruhea	A1
Chandpur	C2	Khulna	C1	Ruppur	C1
Chandraghona	C3	Kishorganj	B2	Saidpur	B1
Chhatak	B2	Kulaura	B3	Sandwip Island	C2
Chiringa	D3	Kurigram	B1	Sangu (river)	D3
Chittagong	C2	Kushtia	C1	Sardah	B1
Chittagong Hill Tracts		Kusiyara (river)	B2, B3	Satkania	C3
(region)	C2, C3	Kutubdia Island	D2	Sherpur	B2
Chuadnaga	C1	Laksham	C2	Sherpur	B1
Comilla	C2	Lalmanir Hat	B1	Sirajganj	B1
Cox's Bazar	D2	Madaripur	C2	South Hatia Island	C2
Dacca (Dhaka)	C2	Madhupur Jungle (forest)	B2	Sripur	B2
Duadkandi	C2	Magura	C1	Sunamganj	B2
Dhaleswari (river)	B1, C2	Maiskhal Island	D2	Sundarbans (region)	D1, D2
Dinajpur	B1	Matamuhari (river)	D3	Surma (river)	B2
Durgapur (Susang)	B2	Maulvi Bazar	B2	Susang, see Durgapur	
Faridpur	C1	Meghna (river)	B2	Sylhet	B2
Feni	C2	Mymensingh	B2	Tangail	B1
Feni (river)	C2	Naogaon	B1	Tista (river)	B1
Gaibanda	B1	Narayanganj	C2	Zopui	C3
Ganges (Padma) (river)	C2, C3	Naria	C2		
Ganges, Mouths of the		Nator	B1		
(river mouth)	D1, D2	Nawabganj	B1		

113

MINI-FACTS AT A GLANCE

GENERAL INFORMATION

Official Name: *Gana Prajatantri Bangladesh* (People's Republic of Bangladesh)

Capital: Dhaka. Spelling was changed officially from Dacca to Dhaka in 1983.

Government: Bangladesh is a multiparty republic with one legislative house, *Jatiya Sansad* (Parliament). The prime minister is head of the government. Three hundred thirty members of the Parliament are elected for a five-year term; thirty seats are reserved for women; the women members are appointed by the ruling party. Villages are the smallest units of local government. Administratively the country is divided into 4 divisions and 64 districts.

Religion: Islam is the official religion. Almost 87 percent of the population is Muslim; some 12 percent are Hindu. Christianity and Buddhism are the other religions.

Ethnic Composition: Bengali is the largest group consisting of some 98 percent of the population; the next largest group is Bihari (Indian Muslims who moved to Bangladesh from the Indian state of Bihar at the time of partition in 1947). Less than one million people belong to tribes such as Chakma, Tippera, Garo, Khasi, and Santhal.

Language: Bengali is the official language spoken by some 95 percent of the population. Derived from Sanskrit, it is an ancient language. Since independence, more and more stress has been given to Bengali and as the direct result, there has been a decline in the use of English.

National Flag: The national flag is green with a red disc in the center. The green of the flag is inspired by the country's association with Islam; it also stands for scenic beauty. Blood shed during the struggle for freedom is recalled by the red disc.

National Emblem: A seven-petaled *shapla* (water lily) rising from five wavy lines (reflecting Bengali rivers) is enclosed within two shoots of paddy. On the top are four stars (reflecting economic and social goals) and a cluster of three jute leaves.

National Anthem: "Amar Sonar Bangla" ("My Golden Bengal")

National Calendar: Gregorian

Money: The taka (T) of 100 paisa is paper currency. It is on the same monetary scale as the Indian rupee. In 1991 one Bangladesh taka was worth $.03 in United States currency.

Membership in International Organizations: Asian Development Bank (ADB); Organization of the Islamic Conference (OIC); South Asian Association of Regional Cooperation (SAARC); World Bank; World Health Organization (WHO); British Commonwealth, Colombo Plan

Foreign Aid: Bangladesh is heavily dependent on large amounts of foreign aid. With widespread problems like poverty, malnutrition, underemployment, rapidly increasing population, and frequent natural disasters, foreign aid is crucial and has often made the difference in the nation's survival. The total foreign aid in 1990-91 amounted to $1,800 million.

Weights and Measures: The metric system was introduced in 1982, but the imperial system of measure is still in use.

Population: 116,600,000 (July 1991 estimates); distribution is 76 percent rural and 24 percent urban. The density is 2,032 persons per sq. mi. (784 persons per sq km)—one of the highest in the world.

Cities:

Dhaka	2,365,695
Chittagong	1,391,877
Khulna	437,304
Rajshahi	253,740
Mymensingh	190,911
Comilla	184,132
Barisal	172,905
Sylhet	168,371
Rangpur	153,174
Jessore	148,927

(Population figures based on 1981 census.)

GEOGRAPHY

Border: The border is shared with India (1,605 mi./2,583 km) and Burma (145 mi./233 km).

Coastline: 357 mi. (575 km) along the Bay of Bengal

Land: Bangladesh is basically a large delta known as the Lower Indo-Gangetic Plain except the Chittagong Hill Tracts region in the extreme southeast. Most of the country lies barely above sea level. Its soil consists mostly of fertile alluvium. Small islands, called *chars*, dot the offshore delta areas in the Bay of Bengal. The coastal land east of the Padma-Meghna Delta is known as the *Sundarbans,* a mix of swampy land, water, and forests where tigers are common.

Highest Point: Mount Keokradong at 4,034 ft. (1,230 m)

Lowest Point: Sea level

Rivers: Bangladesh has one of the most complex river systems in the world. There are some 700 rivers. There are 3 principal river systems. The Jamuna-Brahmaputra flows from the north and meets the Ganges forming the Padma River not far from Dhaka. The Meghna flows from the northeast border with India until it meets the Padma. Eventually all waters flow southward into the Bay of Bengal. The courses of these rivers often shift because the land is so flat. This causes great loss of human and animal life. The flooding of rivers is an annual event.

Forests: Some 15 percent of the land is forested. Most of the forested area is in the Chittagong Hill Tracts region. Teak is an important product. Elephants are employed in moving and hauling timber from the dense forests. Forests are rapidly being cut down mainly for use as fuel. This drastic loss of woodlands has resulted in more severe flooding. Bangladesh's landscape is dotted with palm, bamboo, mango, tamarind, and flowering trees. The mangroves of the Sundarbans are the largest stand of these trees found anywhere in the world. The mangrove trees are used both for timber and firewood.

Wildlife: Large crocodiles (three times the size of humans) live in the Sundarbans. Pythons, tigers, storks, monkeys, spotted deer, clouded leopards, monitor lizards, bears, and wild pigs are found in the forests. The famous royal Bengal tiger is found in the Sundarbans. Bird life consists of many varieties of birds, pheasants, and waterfowl. The Asian elephant and Bengal tiger are considered endangered species.

Climate: Located on the Tropic of Cancer, Bangladesh has a tropical monsoon climate that is often marked with extremes. Temperatures are quite mild throughout the year. April and May are the hottest months. The brief winter lasts from December to January. The rainy season is from June to September when the country receives from 55 in. to 235 in. (140 cm to 597 cm) of rainfall. Humidity is high throughout the year. Periodic cyclones are devastating for human life and the economy of the country.

Greatest Distance: North to south — 464 mi. (747 km)
East to west — 288 mi. (463 km)

Area: 55,598 sq. mi. (143,998 sq km)

ECONOMY AND INDUSTRY

Agriculture: About 70 percent of the land is under cultivation, and another 5 percent is meadows and pastures. Although Bangladesh ranks among the leading rice-growing countries in the world, the rice yield per acre is among the lowest. Rice is grown and harvested 3 times a year in some areas. Jute is the chief cash crop, often called the "golden" crop. Almost 75 percent of the country's export earnings come from jute. Bangladesh is the largest jute producer in the world. Jute is used for rope and twine, for carpet backing and carpeting, and for industrial-quality sacks. Tea is grown in the northeast in the Sylhet Hills region. Other crops are sugarcane, tobacco, wheat, bananas, oilseeds, spices, jackfruit, mangoes, and pineapples. The farms are fragmented and very small; an average farm is about 3.5 acres (1.5 hectares). Cattle, goats, water buffalo, and sheep are the chief livestock. Most of the cattle are undernourished and do not produce much milk. Bangladesh is a leading supplier of animal hides and skins. People living in the countryside fish daily for food during the flood season. Bangladesh exports a large amount of seafood (shrimp and frog legs) to Japan.

Mining: Mineral resources are few. However, there are large deposits of natural gas and smaller deposits of coal and petroleum. Other minerals include marine salt and limestone. Energy is derived principally from natural gas.

Manufacturing: Jute products, leather, paper and paper products, textiles, chemical fertilizers, cement, iron and steel, yarn, soaps and detergents, glass, and electric fans are the chief manufactured products. With the help from *Grameen* (Village) Bank, small loans are given generally to poor women to start a small business. Recently the garment industry has become very successful in Bangladesh where more than 300,000 people, mostly women, are employed by several small-scale factories. Bangladesh is the fourth-largest supplier of cotton garments to the U.S. One unusual occupation is the dismantling of ships near the port of Chittagong. An export processing zone (EPZ) has been established in Chittagong. Handicrafts include weaving of jute and silk, embroidery, pottery, woodenware, and articles of brass, copper, gold, and silver.

Transportation: Boats are the most common means of transportation in the countryside. Small boats carry people and goods across the numerous small rivers. Also, during the rainy season travel by boat is the only way to get around in Bangladesh. There are some 300,000 country boats and some 5,000 mi. (8,047 km) of navigable waterways. Steamers and barges are used for longer trips and to carry heavy loads. Chittagong is the nation's chief seaport. There are about 1,785 mi. (2,873 km) of railway tracks, and almost 7,000 mi. (1,127 km) of roads out of which a very small amount is paved. Road building is expensive and difficult as numerous bridges are needed across rivers. Bicycle rickshaw is the most common mode of transportation in the cities. There are some 180,000 bicycle rickshaws in Bangladesh. The major international airport is at Dhaka; Biman Bangladesh is the official airline.

Communication: There are some 65 daily newspapers in Bengali and English. The radio and television stations are owned by the government. Also, all postal and telecommunications services are controlled by the government. Both Western shows and traditional Bengali cultural programs are popular on TV. Reading of the Koran, Islam's holy book, is shown daily.

Trade: Chief imports are minerals, textiles, vegetable products, machinery, chemicals, transport equipment, and edible oils. Major import sources are the United States, Japan, India, Singapore, Great Britain, China, and Hong Kong. Bangladesh exports cotton textiles, ready-made garments, prawns and shrimps, leather and leather products, raw jute and jute products, and tea; chief export destinations are the United States, Italy, Singapore, Great Britain, Germany, Japan, and Belgium.

EVERYDAY LIFE

Health: Basic health services are relatively undeveloped. Life expectancy at between 50 to 55 years is one of the lowest in the world. Diseases of the respiratory system (tuberculosis), infectious intestinal diseases, cholera, leprosy, malaria, diarrhea, and malnutrition are widespread. During the 1980s there were some government efforts to reduce the high birth rate. The infant mortality rate is one of the highest in the world.

Education: Education is not compulsory, but primary education for five years is provided free by the government. Most of the villages have religious schools and some kind of an elementary school. The primary school is for children from age 6 to 10, and secondary school is from age 11 to 17. There are some 200 vocational and teacher-training schools. Higher education is provided by seven universities, including one for agriculture, one for Islamic studies, and one for engineering. Dhaka University, established in 1921, is the largest. The Bangla Academy sponsors translations of scientific and literary works into Bengali. It also maintains an excellent research collection. Bangladesh has one of the lowest literacy rate in the developing countries. In the early 1990s the literacy rate was about 20 percent; male literacy is almost double the female literacy rate.

Holidays:

New Year's Day, January 1
National Mourning Day (Shaheed Day), February 21
Independence Day, March 26
May Day, May 1
National Revolution Day, November 7
Victory Day, December 16
Christmas, December 25

Movable religious holidays include Good Friday, Jamat Wida, Shab-i-Raat, 'Id-al-Fitr, 'Id-al-'Adha, and Durga Puja. Ramadan is the holiest time of the Islamic year. For a whole month people do not eat or drink during the entire day, but eat during the night.

Family and Culture: Islam influences food, marriage customs, and family relationships in Bangladesh. Marriages are almost always arranged by the parents; a Muslim man may have up to four wives at a time. Muslim women in general avoid social contact with men who do not belong to their family. Muslims are required to pray 5 times a day facing Mecca—Islam's holiest city. Hindus are divided into various social groups called *castes*. Intermarriage between castes is rare.

Though few Bengalis are literate, they have great love of oral traditional literature and poetry. Bengali literature has flourished for hundreds of years in the form of stories and folk ballads. Sir Rabindranath Tagore and Kazi Nazrul Islam are the two most prominent Bengali writers. Religious festivals and social activities are organized by various Muslim, Hindu, Buddhist, and Christian associations. Traditional pottery and fabric are popular among tourists. Dhaka's best-known sight is the Shahid Minar, a monument to those who died in the language riots of 1952. Other sights are the unfinished Lalbagh Fort, Dhaka Museum, and several mosques. The Rajshahi Museum contains artifacts from the 8th-century Buddhist monastery excavated nearby.

Housing and Clothing: The concept of a bungalow in the West is from the Bengali word *bangla*, meaning "living quarters." Most of the city people live crowded together in small wooden houses. Some wealthy families have large brick homes. Most minority groups live together in distinct neighborhoods in cities. Rural houses are mostly built of bamboo with thatch roofs. Very few houses in rural areas have electricity and running water. Bengali women wear a *sari*—a long piece of plain or printed cloth wrapped around the waist and draped over one shoulder. Men wear loose, traditional, lightweight clothing. Men may also wear Western-style pants and shirts.

Food: Rice is the staple food, eaten every day. Fish is also an important part of the meal. Fish and rice are mostly served together with a spicy sauce. Islam forbids the eating of pork. Wheat is slowly becoming part of the daily diet. Tea is the most popular drink.

Sports and Recreation: The most popular sport is soccer (called "football"). Cricket, a game made popular by the British, is also well liked. Dramas based on religious stories are popular forms of entertainment. Visiting friends and family is the most common leisure-time activity. Religious celebrations are enjoyed by both Muslims and Hindus.

Social Welfare: The government sponsors a social welfare program. It is supplemented by several private welfare organizations. In general families take care of their old and sick relatives.

IMPORTANT DATES

1202—Turkish rule is established in the Bengal region

1576—Dhaka is conquered by the Mughal Emperor Akbar

1600—British East India Company is formed

1690—Calcutta city is founded by the British East India Company

1704—Provincial capital of Bengal is moved to Murshidabad

1757—Siraj ud Daulah, the governor of Bengal, is defeated by Robert Clive, an official of the British East India Company

1857—The Indian (Sepoy) Mutiny takes place near Delhi

1858—The British government takes over the British East India Company

1885—The Indian National Congress is organized

1905—The province of Bengal is divided into two sections, East Bengal and West Bengal

1906—The All-India Muslim League is formed

1911—The Province of Bengal is reunited

1919—The Government of India Act is passed

1930—The idea of a Muslim state is proposed by Muhammad Iqbal and promoted by the leader of the Muslim League, Muhammad Ali Jinnah

1946—General elections are held in pre-partitioned India

1947—Indian Independence Act is passed in the British House of Commons; on the basis of religion, the former British empire is divided into India and Pakistan; Pakistan consists of two separate provinces East and West Pakistan separated by almost 1,000 mi. (1,609 km) of Indian territory

1948—Founder and first leader of Pakistan, Muhammad Ali Jinnah, dies

1952—Serious language riots take place when Urdu is declared the official language of Pakistan

1954—Bengali is made a joint official language of Pakistan

1958—Ayub Khan becomes president of Pakistan

1963—Severe cyclones devastate human life and crops

1965—Severe cyclones occur

1966—Sheikh Mujibur Rahman, leader of the Awami League, is arrested

1969—Political power is turned over to General Yahya Khan in Pakistan

1970—Severe cyclone and flooding kill about 250,000 people; Awami League wins the national elections; President Yahya Khan postpones the opening of the National Assembly; Awami League launches province-wide agitation in East Pakistan

1971—Sheikh Mujibur Rahman is arrested and imprisoned in West Pakistan; Awami League is outlawed; martial law is declared in East Pakistan; Pakistani army ruthlessly crushes the national movement by killing more than a million Bengalis; some 10 million Bengali refugees flee across the border to India; Awami League declares independence for East Pakistan as the People's Republic of Bangladesh ("Bengal Nation"); India fights side by side with Bangladesh Liberation Army (the "Mukti Bahini"); Pakistani forces surrender to Indian military; country of independent Bangladesh is born

1972—Sheikh Mujibur Rahman is released from Pakistani prison; he is sworn as prime minister of independent Bangladesh; the country is declared to be a secular state and a parliamentary democracy; Treaty of Friendship and Cooperation is signed with India; Bangladesh joins the British Commonwealth; Pakistan withdraws from the commonwealth; the taka is introduced as the national currency; all banks and Pakistani-owned industries are nationalized

1973—First general elections are held; Wildlife Preservation Act is passed

1974—State of emergency is declared; fundamental rights are suspended; Pakistan recognizes Bangladesh; Mujibur Rahman visits Islamabad (Pakistan's capital); India-Bangladesh border is ratified; Bangladesh joins the United Nations

1975—Rahman abolishes parliamentary system of government and establishes a dictatorship with himself as president; Rahman and most of his family are killed in a military coup; army chief of staff General Zia-ur Rahman emerges as a strong leader

1976—Elections are postponed

1977—Zia-ur Rahman becomes president; a referendum is held; three political parties are banned; by an amendment in the constitution, Islam and not secularism, is accepted as the basic principle; Environmental Pollution Control Board is established

1978—Zia-ur Rahman is elected president for a five-year term; refugee pact is reached with Burma

1979—Nationalist party led by President Rahman wins parliamentary elections;

martial law is lifted; Bangladesh starts exporting cotton garments; border demarcation agreement is signed with Burma; the Grameen Bank is started

1981—President Zia-ur Rahman is killed in a military coup in Chittagong

1982—Lieutenant General Hussain Mohammad Ershad installs himself as martial law administrator; National Assembly and constitution are suspended

1983—Dacca is renamed Dhaka by an official decree; Ershad names himself president; South Asian Association for Regional Cooperation (SAARC) is established

1985—Ershad enforces ban on political parties; opposition leaders are jailed; severe cyclone strikes Bangladesh taking more than 11,000 lives

1986—The first summit conference of SAARC is held in Bangladesh; martial law is lifted and general elections take place; a bilateral investment treaty is signed with the U.S.; government adopts a policy of "Health for All"

1987—President Ershad receives the United Nation's Population Award for his work to reduce the high birth rate in Bangladesh

1988—Severe floods destroy several hundred bridges, kill more than 2,000 people, and leave about 25 million people homeless; Islam becomes the state religion

1990—President Ershad is forced to resign and is imprisoned on fraud charges; monsoon floods affect some 500,000 people; Bangladesh sends 2,300 men to Saudi Arabia to join the multinational forces against Iraq; thousands of Bangladeshis working in Kuwait and Iraq become refugees and must be brought home

1991—Severe cyclone hits Bangladesh killing some 140,000 people; general elections take place, Begum Khalida Zia of the Nationalist party is elected the prime minister; U.S. writes off $300 million of Bangladesh's debt

1992—Tens of thousands of refugees, mostly Muslims, forced out of neighboring Burma pour into Bangladesh

IMPORTANT PEOPLE

Muhammad Ayub Khan (1907-74), Pakistani politician; initiated agrarian, political, and economic reforms

Robert Clive (1725-74), British East India Company official, helped establish empire of British India

Captain Hiram Cox, an English army officer; wrote an 8-volume journal of a residence in the Burman Empire in the nineteenth century; settled the region where Cox's Bazar, the resort city named after him, is located

Indira Gandhi (1917-84), Indian politician, prime minister of India from 1966 to 1977, and again from 1980 to 1984

Mohandas K. Gandhi (1869-1948), Indian nationalist, often called Father of India, led the nonviolent freedom movement against the British

Major General Hussain Mohammad Ershad (1930-   ), military leader of Bangladesh during the 1980s

George Harrison (1943-   ), one of the Beatles (music group) sponsored a live concert at Madison Square Garden in New York City to aid people of Bangladesh in 1971

Sheikh Hasina Wajed, daughter of Sheikh Mujibur Rahman, and current leader of the opposition Awami League party

A.K. Fazlul Haq (1873-1962), former premier of Bengal province, dominated Bengali politics for half a century

Sir Muhammad Iqbal (1877-1938), Indian poet and philosopher, called for separate Muslim state in 1930

Kazi Nazrul Islam, Bengali poet and writer, known as the voice of Bengali nationalism

Muhammad Ali Jinnah (1876-1948), Indian politician, called for separate Muslim state; first governor-general of Pakistan from 1947 to 1948; considered "father" or founder of Pakistan

Begum Khalida Zia, widow of General Zia-ur Rahman and also the leader of the Bangladesh Nationalist party; prime minister of Bangladesh since 1991

Lord Louis Mountbatten (1900-79), British naval hero and member of the royal family; last viceroy of India; supervised the partition of India and Pakistan

Sheikh Mujibur Rahman (1920-75), Bengali politician, often called Father of the Nation; a leader of the Awami League, led the successful fight for the independence of East Pakistan; also the first prime minister of Bangladesh from 1972 to 1975

Khandakar Mushtaq Ahmed (1918-   ), installed as president in 1975 when Mujibur Rahman and his family were assassinated

Siraj ud Daulah (1732-57), governor of Bengal 1756-57; defeated by Robert Clive

Sir Rabindranath Tagore (1861-1941), the best-known Indian Bengali poet; author of the Bangladesh National Anthem "Our Golden Bengal"; received Noble Prize for Literature in 1913

H.S. Suhrawardy (1893-1963), former premier of Bengal, also briefly premier of Pakistan

Yahya Khan (1917-80), professional soldier, president of Pakistan from 1969 to 1971

Dr. Mohammad Yunus, professor of economics at the Chittagong University; started the idea of Grameen Bank to uplift the rural poor; his idea has been adopted in several African countries and even in the United States

Major General Zia-ur Rahman (1936-81), military ruler of the country from 1976 until his assassination in 1981

INDEX

Page numbers that appear in boldface type indicate illustrations

About the Author

Jason Lauré was born in Chehalis, Washington, and lived in California before joining the United States army and serving in France. He attended Columbia University and worked for *The New York Times*. He traveled to San Francisco and became a photographer during the turbulent 1960s. He recorded those events before setting out on the first of many trips to foreign countries experiencing their own turmoil. The first of these, in 1971, was to East Pakistan, which was in the process of becoming the new nation of Bangladesh.

He trekked from Calcutta, to Bangladesh with one of the first groups of refugees returning to their homeland and stayed on to record the triumph and tragedy facing them. He returned a few years later to capture the lives of the children for a book about the birth of Bangladesh, written in collaboration with Ettagale Blauer. That book, published by Farrar, Straus & Giroux Inc., was nominated for a National Book Award.

Mr. Lauré now adds Bangladesh to his other titles in the Enchantment of the World series: Zimbabwe, Zambia, and Angola.

Mr. Lauré is married to Marisia Lauré, a translator.